TRUTH

STANDING
ON ITS HEAD

INSIGHT FOR
AN EXTRAORDINARY
CHRISTIAN WALK
from the
Sermon on the Mount

Praise for T꞉ꞅꞇꞇ Standing on Its head

"John Day's book, *Truth Standing on Its Head*, is a very provocative study of Our Lord's Sermon on the Mount. The exposition of the Beatitudes and the exhortation based on them is very arresting: it grabs us and demands our attention. The rest of the book continues with the same energy and thrust. The break with previous tradition, and with our own comfortable presuppositions, is rather merciless, but the uncompromising exposition of the new ethic ultimately drives us to the Cross, where our own failings can be exchanged for the righteousness of Christ."

Robert E. Longacre, Professor Emeritus
The University of Texas at Arlington

"John Day has presented an engaging exposition of Jesus' most famous discourse, the Sermon on the Mount. John blends his own careful study of Matthew 5-7 and scholarly research into a book that is replete with practical applications for God's people. The book is well suited for readers who want to dig deeper into the teachings of Jesus and their relevance for today."

Carl Laney, Professor of Biblical Literature
Western Seminary, Portland, OR

"A whole lot of energy goes into making the Bible more *relevant*, but through this exposition of the Sermon on the Mount, John Day makes it clear that Jesus needs no PR firm to help Him find a voice in the twenty-first century. How very timely this two-thousand-year-old sermon sounds today. And how refreshing to encounter this faithful, interesting, insightful, and convicting exposition of the world-changing, paradigm-shifting, expectation-shattering teaching Jesus proclaimed to those who would be His followers. *Truth Standing on Its Head* is a reminder that the most famous sermon ever preached still calls us to radical discipleship."

Jeremy Smith, Executive Minister
First Presbyterian Church, Jackson, MS
Managing Editor, reformation21 (www.reformation21.org)

"The Sermon on the Mount includes some of Jesus' greatest, most practical words—words about spirituality, purity, influence, adultery, loving one's enemies, giving, prayer, boasting, worry, wisdom, and other topics. In his insightful, easy-to-read exposition of Matthew 5-7, Dr. Day discusses these topics in simple, yet sublime concepts. This excellent book can help guide readers into God's way of looking at life."

Roy B. Zuck, Editor
Bibliotheca Sacra

"For the Christian, navigating life and following Jesus requires first of all reading the seemingly odd map he drew for us. Fortunately, in our explorations, we can use the keys provided by Pastor John Day to read the map and advance on. *Truth Standing on Its Head* helps us take our bearings, persevere, and make the walk with confidence."

Mirela DeLong, Editor
LOGOS, Romania

"During these times and in this culture of seeking self or relying upon one's own goodness, truly seeking God and relying upon His grace has been largely lost. We are not called to a life of religion, but one of love and obedience.

"This book directs us back to our relationship with God by looking deeply into the mind, words, and life of Jesus Christ. Jesus speaks directly to issues of the heart, which apply to our culture and churches today.

"If you struggle in your spiritual pilgrimage or just want to strengthen your spiritual walk, you will find this to be a thorough and carefully written practical guide for addressing the challenges you face today and deepening your relationship with our Lord.

"This book is not for the faint-hearted, but for those who truly seek the living God, are courageous enough to face themselves to seek the truth, and are willing to live in humble obedience to Him. Freedom does not come through the way of the world, but through God's perfect way, love, and mercy."

Glenn Beckwith, SE Asia Regional Director,
Mission to Unreached Peoples

"Here is a book that asks, as Jesus asked, 'Are you hungry? What do you ache for?' How we answer these questions, how we try to satisfy our hunger and aches, will dictate what we do with our lives. This is exactly where *Truth Standing on Its Head* comes in: wise counsel for those who hunger for righteousness and ache to see God. Read it and live it."

Eric Irwin, Pastor
Covenant Presbyterian Church, Issaquah, WA

"I heartily recommend these sermons on the Sermon on the Mount by my friend and fellow pastor, John Day. Dr. Day is a careful scholar who has succeeded in providing an accurate interpretation of the Lord's bracing words, faithful to their historical and Biblical context. He is an able communicator whose own exposition is clear and easily sustains the reader's interest. And he is a wise and understanding pastor who applies the text in very helpful ways to our modern life. No Christian can be too familiar with the Lord's great sermon."

Rev. Dr. Robert S. Rayburn, Senior Minister of
Faith Presbyterian Church, Tacoma, WA
Stated Clerk of the Pacific Northwest Presbytery (PCA)

"In this splendid exposition of the Sermon on the Mount, John Day exhibits his gifts as both scholar and pastor. The text is handled with technical expertise but is never left as a mere specimen of exegetical method. Rather, the work is winsomely sermonic, constantly in touch with today's real world and its needs. I highly commend it to pastors and other church leaders as well as serious laity eager to mine the Sermon on the Mount for all its golden nuggets."

Eugene H. Merrill, PhD, Distinguished
Professor of Old Testament Studies, Dallas Theological Seminar

"John Day writes well. He makes the Sermon on the Mount alive, relevant, and reflective. This is a GOOD read. Just do it!"

Rex A. Koivisto, ThD, Professor of Biblical and
Theological Studies, Multnomah University, Portland, OR

"In clear, readable prose, John Day moves carefully through the Sermon on the Mount, showing how it embodies Jesus' paradoxical fulfillment of the law. Practical and pastoral, *Truth Standing on Its Head* will both encourage and convict, and point the student to the hard and happy way of obedient discipleship."

Peter J. Leithart, author, Dean of Graduate
Studies and Senior Fellow, New Saint Andrews College, Moscow, ID

"Every Christian in the United States should read *Truth Standing on Its Head* by Pastor John Day. The gloss of our culture so obfuscates Christian values that even the most devout among us could profitably make use of this penetrating roadmap in their daily lives. Structured around the teachings of Jesus in the Sermon on the Mount, Pastor Day, a Biblical scholar, uses informal language and simple contemporary examples to illustrate profound Biblical truths that are not readily apparent. A great guide for focusing on the essentials of the faith in our complex society."

Mike Liles, Jr., Author,
Christian Faith in Contemporary Society: The Framework for Belief

"Most of us have felt perplexed at one time or another reading the paradoxes of the Sermon on the Mount in Matthew 5-7. What did Jesus mean when He said, 'Blessed are the persecuted'? How can it be a happy thing to be hurting? *Truth Standing on Its Head* is a book that will help answer your questions. With careful and responsible study, Dr. John Day shows what he rightly calls the "mind-expanding and life-changing" relevance of Jesus' Sermon. This book will be a welcome addition to my library as I prepare to preach on Matthew 5-7. Yet, it is written in a way that is clear and accessible to all readers. It is well suited for small group Bible studies or for personal devotions."

Chris Brauns, Author,
Unpacking Forgiveness: Biblical Answers for Complex Questions and Deep Wounds
Pastor, The Red Brick Church, Stillman Valley, IL

"This book strongly challenges our modern complacent lifestyles, but does so in a gentle, pastoral way. It digs deep into the meaning of the Scripture, but makes it accessible to everyone. I felt like I listened to a year's worth of excellent sermons."

Allen Pritzlaff, missionary to Central Asia,
speaker on ministry to Muslims

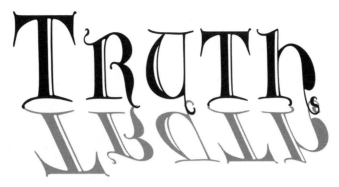

Standing
on Its head

Insight for an
Extraordinary Christian Walk
from
The Sermon on the Mount

John N. Day

Ventura, California
2009

Truth Standing on Its Head:
Insight for an Extraordinary Christian Walk from the Sermon on the Mount

by John N. Day

Copyright © 2009 by John N. Day

john.day@bellewoodpc.com

International Standard Book Number: 978-0-9824929-3-2

Library of Congress Control Number: 2009940534

Theology Editor: Ronald W. Kirk

Manuscript Editors: Mary-Elaine Swanson
and Kimberley Winters Woods

Copy editor: Mary Malcolm

Interior Design & Managing Editor: Desta Garrett

Cover Design: Robbie Destocki

"If We Are the Body" by Mark Hall of Casting Crowns. Copyright © 2003 Club Zoo Music (BMI) My Refuge Music (BMI) (adm. by EMI CMG Publishing) / SWECS Music (BMI). All rights reserved. Used by permission.

"Don't Worry, Be Happy" by Bobby McFerrin, 1988 Grammy Best Song. Probnoblem Music. Used by permission.

Larry Norman, "One Way" from the album "In Another Land," 1975. Solid Rock Productions. All rights reserved. Used by permission.

"Gotta Serve Somebody," written by Bob Dylan. Copyright © 1979. Special Rider Music. All rights reserved. International copyright secured. Reprinted by Permission.

Except where otherwise noted, Scripture quotations are taken from The Holy Bible: English Standard Version®, Copyright © 2001 by Crossway Bibles, a publishing ministry of Good News Publishers. Used by permission. All rights reserved.

Scripture quotations marked "NIV" are taken from the Holy Bible, New International Version®. NIV®. Copyright © 1973, 1978, 1984 by International Bible Society. Used by permission of Zondervon. All rights reserved.

Printed in the United States of America.

Published by

 Nordskog Publishing Inc.

Nordskog Publishing, Inc.

2716 Sailor Ave., Ventura, California 93001, USA

1-805-642-2070 • 1-805-276-5129

www.NordskogPublishing.com

MEMBER

 spa

Christian Small Publishers Association

This book is dedicated to

my granddaughter,

Hope.

As I affectionately say:

"It's always good to have Hope."

"...*that through endurance and through*

the encouragement of the Scriptures,

we might have hope."

Romans 15:4

ABOUT THE AUTHOR

JOHN N. DAY is senior pastor of Bellewood Presbyterian Church (PCA) in Bellevue, Washington, where he has served since 1999. He received his PH.D. in Old Testament from Dallas Theological Seminary in 2001, and is the author of *Crying for Justice: What the Psalms Teach Us about Mercy and Vengeance in an Age of Terrorism* (Grand Rapids: Kregel, 2005). His interests include music, gardening, and games. He and his wife Lorri have four children and one grandchild.

PUBLISHER'S
WORD

Paradox is truth standing
on her head to attract attention.

—G. K. Chesterton—

(See chapter 1, page 2.)

FOR over four decades I have heard and read sermons, articles, and books about the great Sermon On the Mount. To the best of my recollection, this book by Dr. John Day, is the best exposition of the doctrine of Christ at His Galilee mountainside teaching and preaching, and we are as delighted to publish it for our own edification as well as yours.

You will be informed and challenged by the author's pastoral care in propounding this paradoxical truth, *Truth Standing On Its Head* (from the world's viewpoint) and by his loving and verse by verse dissection of chapters five, six, and seven from the Gospel of St. Matthew. This is the summation of all the law and the prophets—THE GOSPEL OF JESUS CHRIST. This discourse is considered the Greatest Sermon Ever Told from the Greatest Story Ever Told—His Story. Here are the essential Commandments for His disciples and for all peoples for all times.

"Above all else, guard your heart, for it is the wellspring of life" (Prv 4:23, NIV). While the Old Testament revealed the external actions and requirements of the Law-Word of God, the New Testament, upon Christ's incarnation, more completely reveals the internal. Of course, in this life Jesus' teaching is not fully attainable without the power of the Holy Spirit. For He enables believers through Bible study, prayer, and practice by faith—which is obedience to our Heavenly Father. This is the holiness a Holy Lord requires for a relationship with Him in this life and in the life to come, eternally.

This book will help you cut to the heart of the matter, with Christ's very TRUTH. For He said, "I am the Way, the TRUTH, and the Life. No one man comes to the Father except through Me" (Jn 14:6, emphasis added).

Noah Webster (in his 1828 *American Dictionary**) relates: *sermon (n.)* —a discourse, extemporary address or written, based on Scripture and delivered in public; *sermonize (v.)* to preach; to tutor; to teach by instruction and advice. As an illustration, he quotes Dryden:

His preaching much, but more His practice wrought,
A living sermon of the truths He taught.

A proper sermon is educational and inspiring, and thus should be life-changing. Certainly if we heed the Sermon on the Mount, our lives will be changed and we will become ever more suitable vessels of the gospel and ambassadors of His Kingdom.

The great Puritan commentator, Matthew Henry, in his *Commentary on the Whole Bible*, 1840, said this about the Sermon on the Mount, with the eight Beatitudes—the paradoxes, in Matthew 5:3-12:

It is the longest and fullest continued discourse of our Saviour that we have upon record in all the gospels. It is a practical discourse; there is not much of the credenda of Christianity in it—the things to be believed, but it is wholly taken up with the agenda—the things to be done. These Christ began with in His preaching: for if any man will do His will, he shall know of the doctrine, whether it be of God....

The Preacher was our Lord Jesus, the Prince of preachers, the great Prophet of His church, who came into the world to be the Light of the world. The prophets and John had done virtuously in preaching, but Christ excelled them all. He is the eternal Wisdom, that lay in the bosom of the Father, before all worlds, and perfectly knew His will (Jn 1:18); and He is the eternal Word, by whom He has in these last days spoken to us.

The many miraculous cures wrought by Christ in Galilee ...were intended...to dispose people to receive instructions

* *An American Dictionary of the English Language* by Noah Webster (Facsimile 1828). Chesapeake, VA: Foundation for American Christian Education, 1967, 1995.

from One in whom there appeared so much of a Divine power and goodness; and, probably, this sermon was the summary, or rehearsal, of what He had preached up and down in the synagogues of Galilee.... Repent, for the kingdom of heaven is at hand."

Mr. Henry interestingly also relates in his *Commentary*, so widely read by America's Founding Fathers, the following insights (paraphrased):

The place was a mountain in Galilee, not one of the holy mountains, as the mountains of Zion, but a common mountain.... [A]s it is the will of God that men should pray and preach every where, anywhere, provided it be decent and convenient. Christ preached this exposition of the law on a mountain, because on a mountain the law was given (Mt. Sinai), and this Sermon on the Mount was also a solemn promulgation of the Christian law.

Contrasting the Old with the New Testaments, when the Law (Ten Commandments) were given (to Moses), the Lord came down upon the mountain; now the Lord Jesus went up the mountainside; then God spoke in thunder and lightning; now, in a still small voice; then the people were ordered to keep their distance; now they are invited to draw near (Jesus, the Christ): a blessed change!

Now read on, and learn what Dr. John Day has to tell us, so brilliantly and gently, and with great understanding and wisdom, about Jesus' greatest and longest-recorded sermon. Get your highlighter and pour yourself into TRUTH *Standing On Its Head: Insight for an Extraordinary Christian Walk from the Sermon on the Mount!*

"*And when the Son of man cometh in His glory and the holy Angels with Him, then shall He sit upon the throne of His glory.*" (Mt 25:31)

—Gerald Christian Nordskog
Publisher
November, 2009

CONTENTS

STANDING
ON ITS HEAD

INSIGHT FOR
AN EXTRAORDINARY
CHRISTIAN WALK
from the
Sermon on the Mount

HAPPY AND HUMBLE

(Matthew 5:1-5)

Seeing the crowds, He went up on the mountain,
and when He sat down, His disciples came to Him.
And He opened His mouth and taught them, saying:
"Blessed are the poor in spirit, for theirs is the kingdom of heaven.
"Blessed are those who mourn, for they shall be comforted.
"Blessed are the meek, for they shall inherit the earth." [1]

A LMOST anyone you ask might say sermons are boring. This can be hard news to hear if you are a preacher. It is doubly hard if you find yourself studying this book on our Lord's Sermon on the Mount, which is essentially a series of sermons about a sermon found in Matthew chapters 5-7. But the Sermon on the Mount is far from boring. Many of those who love our Lord's teachings tend to love it most. Whether one is a Christian or not, there is much to be both honored and emulated, for Jesus cuts straight to the heart. He confronts our human tendency toward "image religion" that is based on outward show and selfish attitudes. Jesus crushes our idols, especially those stubborn ones of entitlement and hypocrisy. In doing so, He demonstrates that a genuine relationship with God shows itself in selfless and humble-hearted obedience. It can be a mind-expanding and life-transforming sermon if we will take the time to truly hear.

One of Matthew's concerns is to show how Jesus fulfills the Old Testament. We see Him going up "on the mountain" (5:1), which is Matthew's way of signaling a *new Moses*—one who is greater than Moses. Just as Moses, from the mountain, delivered the ethics of the kingdom in a set

---

1 Unless otherwise noted, all quotations of Scripture throughout this book are taken from The Holy Bible: English Standard Version (Wheaton, IL: Standard Bible Society), 2001.

of Ten Commandments, so now Jesus delivers the ethics of the kingdom in an even deeper way, beginning with a set of Eight Blessings (or *Beatitudes*), the eighth being highlighted with a double blessing.

These Beatitudes, as is the entirety of His sermon, are truly radical words and life-changing. But what things should we notice first as we begin the Beatitudes? Three things stand out: First, this whole sense of paradox that characterizes the Christian life; second, those things that Jesus places first, that are indeed first, and that must always be first; and third, the place where true happiness really dwells and where true happiness is really found.

TRUTH STANDING ON HER HEAD

The Beatitudes appear to be a list of paradoxes. A paradox is a statement of truth that on its face seems contradictory. For example, let us paraphrase the second blessing (verse 4), *happy…are the* un*happy*. These are two things that cannot be true simultaneously, and yet Jesus claims it is so. The Christian life, as Jesus brings it to us, is full of paradox; for example, we die to live. Or, as G. K. Chesterton describes it, "Paradox is truth standing on her head to attract attention."[2] That is a fitting image.

This list of eight blessings I summarize in three basic categories: *happy* and *humble* (5:3-5), *happy* and *hungry* (5:6-8), and *happy* and *harassed* (5:9-12). These are not things we naturally associate with happiness. But this is the startling Christian paradox: Jesus' opposite-world way, and how He brings us into the most blessed and happy life.

I am using the terms *blessed* and *happy* somewhat interchangeably— and I believe rightly so. The Greek term μακάριος on its face means *happy*, and it brings out forcefully the shocking import of what Jesus is saying. What we are to see is not the shallow and transient way we tend to think about happiness, but a deep and abiding happiness—the settled happiness, or *joy*, of those who know they have the favor of the Lord.

My encapsulation of the sense of the first three—poor in spirit, mourning, and meek—is *happy* and *humble*. Why would Jesus call these things blessed, and place them first on His list? We might say instead, "happy

---

2 G. K. Chesterton, "When Doctors Disagree," in *The Paradoxes of Mr. Pond* (New York: Dover Publications, 1990), 35; www.scribd.com/doc/222055/The-Paradoxes-of-Mr-Pond-1937-by-G-K-Chesterton.

are the rich," or "happy are the powerful." The poor do not usually appear to possess anything of real value, and the meek do not naturally gain any territory. But here, according to Jesus, the poor possess the kingdom of heaven, and the meek inherit the earth! That is paradox.

SPIRITUALLY DESTITUTE

So, let us look at what Jesus places first. Jesus begins with an odd phrase: "Blessed are the poor in spirit" (5:3). What does it mean and why is it first?

It is important to notice the *poverty* issue. As we look all around us, we notice in our affluent environment that physical riches often drive one *away from* God. Wealth can become a rival god (see Mt 6:24) which rarely admits a need for God. This is why Jesus says it is so difficult for a rich man to enter the kingdom of heaven (see Mt 19:23). Physical poverty, on the other hand, often drives one *to* God. One of the virtues we all must learn is our day-by-day dependence upon God for all things as we are taught in the Lord's Prayer, "give us *this day* our daily bread" (Mt 6:11).[3]

Jesus is not speaking of a material or unqualified poverty. He is addressing poverty "in spirit." To be poor in spirit is to be spiritually destitute. It is to acknowledge our utter spiritual need for and complete dependency upon God. Indeed, in the Psalms, this kind of poverty is a way of describing the basic sense of spirituality. Over and over, the one who seeks, and knows, and trusts in the Lord, is called "poor and needy." Take, for example, Psalm 86:1-2:

> Incline Your ear, O LORD, and answer me,
> for I am poor and needy.
>
> Preserve my life, for I am godly;
> save Your servant, who trusts in You
> —You are my God.

We see this also classically expressed in Isaiah 57:15, from the lips of our exalted Lord "who inhabits eternity, whose name is Holy: 'I dwell in the high and holy place, *and also* with him who is of a contrite and lowly spirit.'"

---

3 All emphases or italics in Scripture quotations throughout this book are the author's own.

If we want to possess heaven, we can never escape this first necessity. We can never grow out of, or graduate beyond, or be promoted out of being "poor in spirit." It is the fundamental recognition of our need: that we stand before God as sinners, unworthy, unable, naked, and in need of His clothing grace. We all must begin our Christian journey here, and this is the foundation upon which the rest of the Christian life is built. That is why it is listed first among the Beatitudes. Do you have that spirit of humility? Do you have that need for God?

You see, the kingdom of heaven is not granted on the basis of merit or might, which is where the Pharisees and Zealots erred. It is granted to those who come to God knowing they have nothing to offer, who cry out to Him for mercy, and He hears them. It is granted to people who are well aware of their need, such as the poor, or women of ill-repute, or those loathed tax-collectors like Matthew himself (see Mt 9:9). All who would enter the kingdom of heaven must begin here. All who begin here—and continue here—have the blessing of heaven as a present possession. Notice how this focus on the present frames the otherwise future promises (5:3 and 10): "for theirs *is* the kingdom of heaven." It bookends the Beatitudes as a marker of emphasis. Heaven is not something that we are able to attain, but it *is* something we can possess, by His grace.

To be poor in spirit is to come to the place of truly acknowledging our need before God—and never leaving that place. It is there that we find the real and lasting blessings of God.

MOURNING OVER SIN

Next, Jesus says, "Blessed are those who mourn" (5:4). Just as the poverty in verse 3 was an acknowledgment of spiritual need, so here mourning is principally a grieving over our sin. It is our sin that *separates* us from God—what a horrible thing!—but the brokenness of repentance is the path of life. As the Scripture teaches, "A broken and a contrite heart, O God, You will not despise" (Ps 51:17).

Do you grieve over your own personal sins, or are you all right with them? We live in a culture that does not mourn over sin. Instead it minimizes sin, presents sin as the better life, and mocks the one with a contrite heart. But that attitude is like dancing on the deck of the Titanic while mocking those who are rushing to the lifeboats.

How serious are you about your sins? Notice the strength of language in James 4:8-10:

> Draw near to God, and He will draw near to you. Cleanse your hands, you sinners, and purify your hearts, you double-minded. Be wretched and mourn and weep. Let your laughter be turned to mourning and your joy to gloom. Humble yourselves before the Lord, and He will exalt you.

This is the happiness that Jesus is driving at: He is offering the peace and comfort of complete forgiveness plus an endless life in the presence of God!

But our brokenness must go beyond ourselves and our own sins. Do you also grieve over the sins of others? Does it bother you when the world rejects God's laws or when a Christian goes on in flagrant sin? Do you mourn over the societal effects of sin, or even possible effects in a higher realm? Does it grieve you that so many people are rushing like proverbial lemmings to an eternal doom? There are also the larger effects of sin—particularly that specter of death that looms over us all, whether it be by the ravages of war, the murder of innocent children through abortion, or the death of a loved one as when Jesus wept over His friend (Jn 11:35).

Part of the blessing here must surely be *the knowledge* that although an individual or corporate lifestyle of sin is not right—it is Jesus that will make it right. Jesus defeated both sin and Satan at the cross, and still more: "The last enemy to be destroyed is death" (1 Cor 15:26). There is true comfort in these truths.

THE POSTURE OF PIETY

Thirdly, there is Christ's blessing on the meek (5:5). We all have trouble understanding what meekness really means. Surely it means that the essence of meekness, as lived out in our lives, is truly understanding our place as *humans* before Almighty God and our place as *sinners* who have received God's grace. It is from this standpoint of our finitude and our sinfulness that we can, and rightly ought to, respond to others in a spirit of patience, kindness, gentleness, and humility.

Meekness is not weakness, though the world always has and always will look at it that way. The world calls us to seize our selfish interests at the expense of others, but Jesus calls us to "learn of Me; for I am meek and lowly in heart" (Mt 11:29, KJV). Will you respond to the call of the world, or the call of Christ? Which takes greater strength—to strike out and seize, or to restrain and relinquish? Men and women fight this temptation in different ways: for men, this typically comes out in *physical* violence or harshness; for women, this typically comes out in *verbal* violence or harshness. But in either case, it is the same lack of meekness that we must learn to forsake if we are to learn from Him.

While we can get what we want in the world's way, because we can gain little bits of territory, seize a bit of prestige, conquer our own little dominions—whether that be the domination of a relationship, a workplace, or an entire nation—we can never seize true happiness. The ironic paradox is this: the meek, that is the gentle and the humble, will "inherit" the earth! Here, Jesus is quoting from Psalm 37:11, which pointed to the Promised Land, but which finds its fulfillment in something far greater: "a *new heaven* and a *new earth*" that awaits us (Rv 21:1), and all that is within them is ours in Christ! So let us be content to wait upon the Lord.

THE PURSUIT OF HAPPINESS

This is being written as we are about to enter into our July Fourth festivities once again—with "bombs bursting in air"—in which we celebrate the founding of our nation, in the Declaration of Independence from mother Britain on July 4, 1776. In this document, the signers declare "We hold these truths to be self-evident, that all men are created equal, that they are endowed by their Creator with certain unalienable rights, that among these are Life, Liberty, and the pursuit of Happiness."[4] These tenets are central to the American vision. Our nation was founded on these values of life, liberty, and the pursuit of happiness. As it was envisioned by the Founding Fathers, even the pursuit of happiness was a noble call. But that is not what it has become. Rather, in our changing culture, it is an unfettered pursuit of personal happiness. Self-indulgence has been raised to prominence, taking precedence over all other things. Thus, for example, personal happiness takes precedence over that life growing inside of me, or that aging parent we would relegate to a stranger's care. We pursue

---

4 The Declaration of Independence, paragraph 2.

happiness relentlessly; and yet, when we have caught what we pursue, we do not find ourselves happy. We look for happiness in wealth and power and fame, in a new wife, a bigger house, a better car; in "sex and drugs and rock-n-roll." Yet, after we attain these things, happiness itself strangely eludes us. As Saint Augustine noted in the opening words of his *Confessions* some sixteen hundred years ago, "Our hearts find no peace until they rest in you." [5]

True happiness, ironically, is found in Christianity—and this happiness is twofold: it is not just for the future, in heaven, but also in the present, the here and now. We see this in the very tenses of the blessings: *is* and *shall*: "for theirs *is* the kingdom of heaven...for they *shall* inherit the earth" (5:3,5). This is the two-sided coin of the kingdom: *already* and *not yet*. Too often our picture of Christianity is "pie in the sky when you die," but for now, only dullness and drudgery and no fun at all. But this is a horrible perversion. As we are told in the Scriptures, the purpose of all God's commands is: "for our good always" (Dt 6:24). So, the promised blessings of Jesus are happiness *now* and happiness *then*.

If you are looking for real and lasting happiness, you will find it in things such as meekness and mercy. Look around you. The happiest people—the most blessed—are not those with the most possessions or the most money. The happiest people are those who understand grace and live selflessly in service to God and to others. Happy...are the humble. This is the Christian paradox; this is the primary thing and the path to lasting happiness.

---

5 Saint Augustine, *Confessions* (London: Penguin Books, 1961), 21.

Happy and Hungry

(Matthew 5:6-8)

Blessed are those who hunger and thirst for righteousness,
for they shall be satisfied.
Blessed are the merciful, for they shall receive mercy.
Blessed are the pure in heart, for they shall see God.

You have probably heard, and you may have even said it, "God wants me to be happy!" or asked, "doesn't God want me to be happy?" This is typically used as an excuse to get out of a difficult marriage or to engage in some selfish behavior. Yes, God does want you to be happy, but not the way you might think. He wants *true* happiness for you—that "blessedness" that comes from seeking and resting in Him, and in walking in His ways. This is how we were made; this is the path of true happiness.

We looked at the first three Beatitudes under the heading "happy and humble," for it is this distinct sense of humility that characterizes these three—poor, mourning, and meek. This is where we must all begin before God. From this starting point, Jesus moves to that which drives us—our appetite—again, paradoxically saying, "happy are the hungry."

SPIRITUAL HUNGER

Jesus begins this move by making the metaphor explicit: "Blessed are those who hunger and thirst for righteousness" (5:6). The truly happy long for righteousness; it is a spiritual hunger. This is an apt description. Just as Jesus drove home our desperate spiritual need by calling it "poverty" (5:3), so He reveals our deepest spiritual urge by calling it "hunger and thirst." Happy are we if we acknowledge our need for God and cast ourselves upon His grace; and happy are we if our motivating desire is to see God's righteousness filling our lives and filling the world.

Now, nobody *likes* to be hungry, especially when you begin to suffer the effects of a low blood-sugar attack. You become ravenous, you start to shake, feel faint, and develop a headache. But, just like pain, hunger is an unpleasant yet clear indicator that *you are alive*. The only people who do not require food and water are…dead people. The only people who do not crave food and water are…dead people. It is a choice analogy for our spiritual lives. So, ask yourself, are you hungry? Are you thirsty? Surely, if there is no spiritual longing, there is no spiritual life.

But what are we to be "hungry and thirsty" for? What are we to really want? Cool toys, success, respect, a big splash in the world pond? No, Jesus spells it out in a word: "righteousness." What *is* righteousness, other than a big and spiritual-sounding word? Righteousness is what is in line with God's standard of what is right. You could call this "an aching" for "rightness"—and in two directions.

First, it is an aching for personal righteousness: that is, to pursue God, to do what is right in His sight, to do His will from the heart, to see His life transform your life, to become more like Christ by the power of the Holy Spirit. It is this hungering and thirsting after God that we see repeatedly in the Psalms, for example:

> As the deer pants for flowing streams,
> so pants my soul for You, O God (Ps 42:1).

> O God, You are my God; earnestly I seek You;
> my soul thirsts for You;
> my flesh faints for You,
> as in a dry and weary land
> where there is no water (Ps 63:1).

This is a deep—even desperate—urge. But is this deep yearning a part of your life?

But God's concern is not only for our personal righteousness; it is also for societal righteousness—that is, justice and rightness in the broadest sense. In fact, this is one of God's chief concerns. He proclaims it in the prophets: "I, the LORD *love* justice" (Is 61:8). What He loves is contrasted with what He hates:

> I hate, I despise your feasts [that is, your religious worship],
> and I take no delight in your solemn assemblies….

But let justice roll down like waters,
and righteousness like an ever-flowing stream
(Am 5:21,24).

This is where our heart must be, if our heart is to beat in unison with God's. If our Christianity does not *love* righteousness and *live* righteousness, it is nothing more than empty religion and meaningless ritual.

Examine yourself. If you do not have this longing, there is good reason to doubt that you are even alive, spiritually speaking, for this is the very bread and water of Christian life. As Jesus says, *"Seek first* the kingdom of God and *His righteousness"* (Mt 6:33).

HUNGER SATISFIED

The hunger Jesus speaks of, then, is a spiritual hunger that *will* be satisfied. But how?

In one very fundamental sense, it is a hunger that has *already* been satisfied if you have come to Jesus, for Jesus Himself claimed, "I am the bread of life; whoever comes to Me shall not hunger, and whoever believes in Me shall never thirst" (Jn 6:35). This is the deep satisfaction of forgiveness and everlasting life that we possess as Christians. And no one can take it away.

However, there is still the *not yet.* We still live in a fallen world. We have not made it to heaven yet, *but we can smell it!*—in much the same way as when your child comes up to you and says "I'm hungry," and you tell him, "Just a few more minutes; dinner's almost ready," and you can smell the chicken roasting and you know your hunger is going to be satisfied soon. This is our blessing. Jesus tells us, "I'm preparing dinner; wash up and get ready." As 2 Peter tells us: "According to His promise, we are waiting for new heavens and a new earth in which righteousness dwells" (2 Pt 3:13). Our longing for rightness *will not* be fully satisfied until all is made right forever, and "they shall hunger no more, neither thirst anymore" (Rv 7:16). But our confidence is this: our longing *will* be satisfied. Perfect righteousness will be established on the earth—when dinner is finally ready and Jesus returns to usher in eternity.

But there is something more *now.* We are to satiate this hunger and quench this thirst *actively* on a daily basis. Again, this is why Jesus' choice of imagery is so germane. Just as our physical hunger and thirst must be addressed *daily*, so must our spiritual life and our walk with God. It is not something we can just do once a week. Try eating and drinking only on Sunday morning; you will not even last a week before you die of thirst. This is the attitude we are to have for our spiritual lives as well, staying regularly nourished by remaining in prayer and studying His Word, taking it into our own bellies as fuel for our day-to-day living, and seeking to see it spill over into society.

WHAT GOD IS LIKE

Next, Jesus speaks a blessing on those who show mercy (5:7). It is good to begin with definition: What is mercy? Too often we think it is simply having sympathetic *feelings* toward someone or something; and sometimes we think it is simply *doing* something helpful for someone in need. But Biblical mercy is comprised of both: It is *compassion* in *action*; it is, you could say, "feelings, with feet." We see this in Jesus' own example of healing the two blind men who begged Him "Lord, have mercy on us!" And the Gospel tells us, "Jesus in pity touched" and healed them (Mt 20:30-34).

And what does it do? Amazingly, perhaps at least in our thinking, it is this mercy, this compassion in action, that really *reveals* God—not some thunderous display of power or glory. Mercy reveals, like nothing else, what God is like. Indeed, it is one of His primary attributes and chief desires. In Exodus 34:6-7, we read how the Lord passed before Moses and proclaimed His name:

> The LORD, the LORD, a God merciful and gracious, slow to anger, and abounding in steadfast love and faithfulness, keeping steadfast love for thousands, forgiving iniquity and transgression and sin, but who will by no means clear the guilty, visiting the iniquity of the fathers on the children and the children's children, to the third and the fourth generation.

But take notice: In that supreme revelation of God's name, which is also His character, what is listed first? "Merciful and gracious." And God tells us elsewhere in the Scriptures: "I desire mercy, and not sacrifice" (Mt 9:13); and that "mercy triumphs over judgment" (Jas 2:13). In Micah 6:8, what does the Lord require of us? "To do justly, and to love mercy, and

to walk humbly with thy God" (KJV)—just like the Beatitudes thus far.
In what way does it reveal God? It shows God's love to those who do not deserve it. By its very nature, seen especially in such things as forgiveness and kindness, mercy is undeserved. When we get to the conclusion of the first chapter of His sermon and His command to love *our enemies*, Jesus says: "You therefore must be perfect, as your heavenly Father is perfect" (Mt 5:48). The way this edict is rendered in Luke's Gospel, however, is this: "Be *merciful*, even as your Father is *merciful*" (Lk 6:36). God's *perfection* is seen especially in His *mercy*! And this calling to be merciful to those who do not deserve it—even our enemies—reminds us that God was first merciful to us when we did not deserve it, for we were once His enemies! It was God's mercy that was shown to us on the cross (see Rom 5:8).

Mercy brings Christ's touch to those who need it: the wounded, the weary, the downcast, the weak. As the apostle Paul tells us, we are the body of Christ: His head, His heart, His hands, His feet. We are the "Jesus" that people will see, and how people see Jesus will depend upon how we interact with them. Will we be perceived as merciful? A few years ago the Christian band, Casting Crowns, had a hit single that asked the question, pointedly and rightly, in the face of the inaction and judgmentalism so common in the church today:

> *But if we are the Body,*
> *Why aren't His arms reaching?*
> *Why aren't His hands healing?*
> *Why aren't His words teaching?*
>
> *And if we are the Body,*
> *Why aren't His feet going?*
> *Why is His love not showing them*
> *There is a way? Jesus is the way.*[6]

Mercy, like justice, is one of God's chief concerns. But is God's concern our concern? Too often we become focused on "good things" like

---

6 "If We Are the Body" by Mark Hall of Casting Crowns. Copyright © 2003 Club Zoo Music (BMI) My Refuge Music (BMI) (adm. by EMI CMG Publishing)/ SWECS Music (BMI). All rights reserved. Used by permission.

right doctrine and respectable appearances and we lose sight of the utter *necessity* of mercy.

What, again, are the Lord's big three? Justice, mercy, humility (Mi 6:8). Or His big two? Love God, and love your neighbor (Mt 22:36-40). And who is your neighbor? We see this question answered in the Parable of the Good Samaritan: "The one who showed him mercy" (Lk 10:37). My neighbor, then, is the one in need and whose need I can meet. Are your eyes open to the needy—both around you and around the world? And is your heart open to their needs? Are your arms open? For this is where God is really seen. There is an old adage that has been frequently applied to those studying for the pastoral ministry: They will not care how much you know until they know how much you care. True, and true for us all.

INWARD PURITY

Jesus goes on to say, "Blessed are the pure in heart" (5:8). What is meant by this purity? Does it mean absolute sinlessness? Would you claim to be pure in heart? Proverbs 20:9 asks "Who can say, 'I have made my heart pure; I am clean from my sin'?" The answer, of course, is no one! It is impossible to be pure in heart, for Scripture teaches that "the heart is deceitful above all things, and desperately sick" (Jer 17:9). So if that was the meaning, then no one could claim the blessing and we would miss Jesus' point that it is a real blessing meant for real people. Yet Jesus also says: "With man this is impossible, but with God all things are possible" (Mt 19:26).

So what is the definition of a pure heart? Let us go back to Matthew 5:3. Just as the phrase "poor in spirit" is rightly understood as "spiritual poverty," that is, our desperate need for God, so also the phrase "pure in heart" (verse 8) speaks of a "spiritual purity." There are two major aspects to this. First is *regeneration*; that is, a heart that is cleansed by God, once and continually. He is the one who purifies our hearts by faith when we come to Christ, and it is He who purifies us from all unrighteousness when we confess our sins (see Acts 15:9; 1 Jn 1:9). The second aspect is *relationship*; that is, a heart that truly seeks Him and that longs to see Him. The psalmist describes it in language that echoes the words of our Lord,

> Who shall ascend the hill of the LORD?
> And who shall stand in His holy place?

He who has clean hands and a *pure heart,*
    who does not lift up his soul to what is false
    and does not swear deceitfully.
He will receive *blessing* from the LORD
    and righteousness from the God of his salvation.
Such is the generation of *those who seek Him,*
    who seek the face of the God of Jacob (Ps 24:3-6).

It is this dual aspect of cleansed and cleansing, of seeking and seeing, that marks the life of the "pure in heart." Do you have a genuine and living relationship with God where you know the forgiveness of sins, and are you seeking after Him? This is what the Lord Himself seeks and where we find our lives most truly blessed.

INWARD EMPHASIS

This blessing on inward purity finds its natural contrast with those who focus on externals. As God said long ago, "Man looks on the outward appearance, but the LORD looks on the heart" (1 Sm 16:7).

This was seen in Jesus' day, most notably, in the example of the Pharisees and scribes. These were the religious leaders and teachers of the Scriptures whom Jesus repeatedly opposed and denounced for their insistence on strict adherence to ritual and the law—which we might refer to as "religiosity"—while their heart, or "inner man," remained hardened and resistant to God. "You also outwardly appear righteous to others, but within you are full of hypocrisy and lawlessness" (Mt 23:28). We often observe this same issue in the leaders of today's churches. It is the frustration and burden of legalism, works for self-justification, and performance-based religion. But it is interesting to observe whether or not those who live by the rule of external laws are happy. Would you say they are living a "blessed" life? Do you observe the liberty of Christ? (see 2 Cor 3:17; Gal 5:1).

The caricature of dour and dull Christians often comes—and rightly so—from such as these whose main concerns in their Christian walk are the relatively little things that people *do* or *do not do.* Jesus' words to us today would be the same as then, when He said, "You tithe mint and dill and cumin, and have neglected the weightier matters of the law: justice and mercy and faithfulness" (Mt 23:23). In contrast, look at those Christians whose hearts have been made pure before the Lord, and you will find both a genuine brokenness—and joy.

As Jesus will say later on, this "externals mentality" does its good religious things to be seen by men (Mt 6:1ff); but the blessing promised to the pure in heart is "to see God"! Let that sink in...to see God! Psalm 17:15 says,

> As for me, I shall behold Your face in righteousness;
> when I awake, I shall be satisfied with Your likeness.

This is where our satisfaction really lies, in the full and unhindered presence of God, in whose presence "there is fullness of joy" and "pleasures forevermore" (Ps 16:11).

I call the message of this group of verses "happy are the hungry" because the truly happy long for righteousness, for mercy, for purity. When we yearn for such things, we express a distinct hunger for God; and we are only truly happy when we satisfy our hunger in Him. So, let us examine ourselves. Are you hungry and thirsty? What is it that you yearn for? What drives and motivates you? Do you desire true happiness? Many people are driven by self-indulgent pursuits such as pleasure, or wealth, or power, or popularity—but true happiness eludes them. Too often they are riddled with doubt and plagued by discontentment. Others may become fearful, insecure in their ability to hold onto what they have gained. They may have achieved their goals, but they have not attained happiness. Why? Because through His word, God has made it clear that true happiness is attached to *righteousness*, to *mercy*; and to inward *purity*. The truly happy are those who long for all three.

HAPPY AND HARASSED

(Matthew 5:9-12)

Blessed are the peacemakers, for they shall be called sons of God.
Blessed are those who are persecuted for righteousness' sake,
for theirs is the kingdom of heaven.
Blessed are you when others revile you and persecute you
and utter all kinds of evil against you falsely on My account.
Rejoice and be glad, for your reward is great in heaven,
for so they persecuted the prophets who were before you.

JESUS began the Beatitudes in the place where we all must begin if we are to know the love of God and enter His embrace, that is, happy and *humble*. Then Jesus moved toward those things that must drive us and sustain us, the place where our appetite must be: happy and *hungry*. But the place where Jesus ends these living gems is even more surprising. Yet it is the place where we must all be drawn if we are drawn after Christ: happy and *harassed*. How can this be?

THE BLESSING OF PEACE

We all love peace! And it is one of the beautiful blessings that Christ gives to His own: "Peace I leave with you; My peace I give to you. Not as the world gives do I give to you" (Jn 14:27). We understand that Jesus is the source of our peace, but here He adds an unusual twist. He says, "Blessed are the peacemakers" (5:9). His blessing does not rest on those who simply find rest by escaping into some state of detachment from the worries and horrors of this world—no, His blessing is on the *"peacemakers"* not the *"peaceful."* It is something we are required to *do*. This means that peace must be "made"; it does not just operate on its own, like the laws of nature. Peace is an action word; it is a *results* word. But peace cannot be made or achieved in the ways we normally use to get results.

17

For instance, can true peace be forced? Consider the current war-zone between Israel and Hamas, or the recent fighting between Israel and Hezbollah. World leaders can force a cease-fire, but they can never enforce true peace without first changing the hearts of the terrorists, whose tireless intent is the very destruction of Israel. It is interesting to notice, however, that this is the very thing that Jesus does. One of Jesus' own twelve disciples, who was hand-picked, was called Simon "the Zealot" (Lk 6:15). Now, the Zealots were a terrorist group of the first century whose tireless intent was the violent overthrow of that occupying power, Rome, by whatever bloody means possible.

This is instructive for us. We as a nation battle with *the sword* in our own War on Terror. But as Christians, we also battle using prayer, and the witness of our lives and our words open with the Gospel, bearing "the sword of the Spirit" (Eph 6:17). We do so because even a terrorist can be transformed; even a terrorist can become a disciple of Jesus. After conversion, he will no longer *be* a terrorist, but we will know him by the marker of God's grace, as he testifies, "that is what I *was*." This is similar to how the apostle Paul described some in the Corinthian church, saying "that is what some of you *were*" (1 Cor 6:11, NIV). Even today fanatical Muslims are turning to Christ and being transformed by Christ. Is this dangerous, scary? Yes—but wonderful.

PRINCIPLES OF PEACEMAKING

This brings us to some principles for peacemaking. How can we become peacemakers? Here are three fundamentals that you can remember under the acronym of **D-O-E**, that is: *Desire* peace—it must begin in the heart; *Own* grace—for grace received is grace lived; and *Engage* with humility—knowing our own sinfulness and frailty.

First, *Desire* Peace.

Just like any real pattern of activity, it starts with the desire for peace. James notes this same beginning point when he describes the pattern for sin:

> But each person is tempted when he is lured and enticed by his own desire. Then desire when it has conceived gives birth to sin, and sin when it is fully grown brings forth death (Jas 1:14-15).

So also, the pattern for peace must begin in the heart with the conviction that peace—in whatever relationship, in whatever conflict—is a good thing, a desirable thing that I want to see happen. But do you? We might be tempted to skip the first two parts (the *D* and the *O*), and jump straight to the third—*Engage*—where we actually try to tackle and solve the problem. But the fault with this approach is that conflict *always* begins in the heart and you can not really tackle the problem until you come to this understanding. The letter of James goes on to tell us that if there is jealousy and selfish ambition *in your hearts*, disorder and evil will always follow. But "peacemakers who sow in peace raise a harvest of righteousness" (Jas 3:18, NIV). So, if you want to reap the blessings of peace, you must start with the desire for peace. Let us look at this first step—*Desire*—in a couple of key particulars: our marriages and church membership.

Within Our Marriages:

This is to be our most intimate relationship and yet it can also be a breeding ground for conflict. So often—and we are seeing this more and more—marriages disintegrate or explode. Perhaps it is due to one big thing, or maybe it is a pile-up of many small things. Christians are just as susceptible to these problems as others; however, we have something in our favor—the Holy Spirit—and so we can, and must, do better than non-Christians. But the foundational question is this, and it is the first question I typically ask in marriage counseling: Do you want the marriage to work? Do you want it to succeed, to get better? Do you love your spouse? And he or she might answer "I don't know; but I want to." So *desire* is where the resolution must begin. If one partner does not want peace, the other must still pursue it to the best of his or her ability, because Scripture instructs us to "seek peace and *pursue* it" (Ps 34:14).

Within Our Own Church Membership:

Some churches today are populated by cliques and cold shoulders. People gather under the same roof to worship the same God, all the while harboring animosity toward someone across the aisle. They are content to live with that; they have no desire to change. They may not admit it, they may even prefer it that way. However, peace is more than the absence of outright conflict. It is the presence of something fundamentally good in our relationships. Do you want to get along? Do you desire peace? In my denomination,[7] the fifth vow that members must take involves a promise to strive for the purity *and peace* of the church. There is a good reason it is in there.

Second, *Own* Grace.

As Christians, we love grace. But do we understand what grace is? Do you *own* grace? For grace, by its very nature, is something wonderful and yet completely undeserved. The beautiful thing is that God did this for us. He gave us forgiveness; He gave us eternal life. God has showered His grace on us, and He calls us to do the same for others: to internalize grace so that we almost *breathe* forgiveness, *breathe* life. When Christ laid down His life for us, He made peace between God and us. We were separated from Him and, indeed, we were His enemies because of our sin and sinful inclinations (see Col 1:20-22). Christ laid down His life for me. How can I not be willing to lay down my life for my brother, my wife, my co-worker, my neighbor (1 Jn 3:16)? With that attitude of laying down our lives for one another, we can make peace with each other. Remember: grace received is grace lived. Where grace is not lived, grace has not truly been received. The parable of the unforgiving servant in Matthew 18:21-35 shows how even after receiving forgiveness for his great debt, he would not, in turn, forgive his debtor. So whether it is the person next to you in bed, or the person next to you in the pew who has wronged you, do you start with this attitude of grace? Can you confess, *I do not* deserve the blessings I have received, yet God freely gave them to me? Or do you hold onto the thought that the other person does not *deserve* your attempts at reconciliation? Unless you fully understand that you can do nothing to merit God's good favor, how can you truly own grace? And once you grasp that reality, how can you not extend His grace to others? Have you received it into your life? Then it must overflow from your life. For grace that is truly received is grace that is lived.

Third, *Engage* with Humility.

This is the point of contact, the actual interaction. Our instincts, as in any conflict, are going to be either "fight or flight," and our tendencies

---

7 The author's denomination is The Presbyterian Church in America (PCA).

are typically on one side or the other. For example, if you are startled with fear, what is your first reaction? For some it is to turn and run, for others it is to turn and fight. But we must stand against both of these automatic responses, whether the urge to attack or the urge to escape, for neither will make peace. They will only worsen or prolong the conflict. Rather, our approach must be to engage the other person. We must reach out—be the first to make the move—understanding our own frailty, sinfulness, and part in the problem. So let us look at this third step in more detail, as it touches on the examples already broached.

Within Our Marriages:

As Christians, we understand that marriage is something *bigger* than two people living together; marriage is something *better* than simply sharing a house. Marriage has a truly *beautiful* design, transcendent in its ordinariness; for marriage was designed to reflect the relationship between Christ and His church. As the apostle Paul describes it:

> "Therefore a man shall leave his father and mother and hold fast to his wife, and the two shall become one flesh." This mystery is profound, and I am saying that *it refers to Christ and the church.* However, let each one of you love his wife as himself, and let the wife see that she respects her husband (Eph 5:31-33).

When others look at us in our marriages, they should get a glimpse of this beauty. Not perfection, by any means, and not façade, but something real and wonderful. What is our role in the relationship? Husband, if you are Christ to your wife, then you need to *love* your wife—whether you feel like it, or whether she deserves it. You need to hold her up as beautiful and precious, and sacrifice yourself for her good. Wife, if you are the church to your husband, then you need to *respect* your husband—again, whether you feel like it, or whether he deserves it. You need to hold him up as admirable, and adjust your way for his welfare. We are to look beyond our "self" and *for* the other. When both husband and wife esteem each other in this way, they both receive something bigger, better, and beautiful.

When conflict comes, as it invariably will, do you take to heart that you are a sinner too, that you share some part of blame, and that you need to major on your own responsibilities before the Lord? Rather than lashing out or holing up, extending grace to your spouse might be something as simple as saying: "Honey, I love you. And I'm very sorry that I hurt you, I don't mean to do that. You are precious to me."

Within Our Own Church Membership:

When our Lord laid down the protocols for dealing with a believer who sinned against us, He began in a very important place that we too often miss or ignore. He said *first*: talk to him alone (Mt 18:15). Do not wait for him to come to you. Do not sit stewing about it. Do not go talking to others about it, and do not send someone else to go and talk to him. To be a *peacemaker*, you must engage, and engage with humility. Galatians 6:1 calls us to reach out and restore a sinner in a spirit of gentleness, knowing our own frailty. This is how we must live with one another. This is how we will know the blessing of peace: by seeking to *make* peace.

THE BLESSING OF PERSECUTION

The last of the Beatitudes brings us to a strange climax. It is a strange way to end; and it is a strange way to respond. What might we expect instead? Certainly not this: persecution—and to be happy about it! "Blessed are those who are persecuted for righteousness' sake" (5:10). Why does He end this way? How can we respond this way?

Strange as it may seem, this is the culmination of the Beatitudes: the pinnacle of Jesus' opposite-world way to call persecution "blessed." Perhaps it should not surprise us, for we are discovering that we are blessed in what might seem the worst. The complete blessing attached to this last point is the very same as is attached to the first: "for theirs is the kingdom of heaven" (see Mt 5:3 and 10; Mt 5:11-12 are but an expansion). This blessing of attaining the kingdom of heaven "bookends" the Beatitudes; and thus reveals a larger whole: If you follow Jesus, you will grow in all of these areas; and the Christian life leads to persecution, just as surely as it leads to heaven.

As mentioned earlier, this is the only Beatitude that gets expanded on—and it appears to get worse. Not only "blessed," but "rejoice" and "be glad"! In some way, we are supposed to be *especially* happy about it! How can this be? Against all of our natural inclinations, we are not to become infuriated, nor retaliate, but rejoice! How is it possible to react to persecution this way? In Matthew 5:12, there are two things that Jesus mentions: (1) "for your reward is great in heaven," and (2) "for so they persecuted the prophets who were before you." They are: (1) because we have a *great reward*; and (2) because we are in *great company*.

Ours is the kingdom of heaven! There is so much more beyond; much greater and lasting joy. So we can hold lightly to this world and this flesh. As the apostle Paul describes it: "The sufferings of this present time are not worthy to be compared with the glory" that awaits (Rom 8:18); and "this light momentary affliction is preparing for us an eternal weight of glory beyond all comparison" (2 Cor 4:17)!

If we suffer for Jesus, it is a badge of honor, for we are following in the footsteps of the saints before us, and they are big shoes to fill. Indeed, the shoes get bigger still. In Hebrews 11, the saints and prophets who suffered before us are paraded as examples of suffering and faith. But then the great cloud of witnesses gives way to a focus on one Person: our Lord and Savior Jesus Christ, "who for the joy that was set before Him endured the cross" (Heb 12:2). Our Lord never calls us to follow where He has not first gone; and where He goes, joy unspeakable must follow.

PRINCIPLES OF PERSECUTION

Just as there are principles of peacemaking, so there are principles of persecution. And there are two that stand out from these words of our Lord. First, it is *inevitable*. Jesus says, "When..." (5:11). The Scriptures promise: "All who desire to live a godly life in Christ Jesus will be persecuted" (2 Tm 3:12); or, as Jesus says in the Gospel of John, "If they persecuted Me, they will also persecute you" (Jn 15:20). Now, this can be subtle and small, such as we experience in America in name-calling and ostracism, or overt and violent like so many places around the world. But the adage holds true: If you are not bumping into Satan, perhaps you are walking with him.

We are used to hearing about the persecution of the early church, how Christians were thrown to the lions and burned at the stake, like the second-century martyrdom of John's disciple, Polycarp. But relative to the entire history of the Christian church, there has also been massive persecution of Christians in this last century, though generally far from us here in the West. We are somewhat protected because of the Christian underpinnings of our nation, although they are being increasingly eroded. But extreme persecution in horrible ways is a common occurrence in many other nations of the world. We hear, for example, of the recent accounts of rape and child slavery in Pakistan, the beheadings of three Christian school-girls in Indonesia, the massacre of Christians in the Sudan, the gory murders of a Christian missionary, pastor, and Muslim convert in Malatya, Turkey, and numerous other such incidents.

But the paradox of persecution is this: the church grows. One notable example is China. Just as in the early centuries, in the testimony of Tertullian, "the blood of the martyrs is the seed of the church." [8] After the foreign missionaries were all expelled, the church had to stand on its own, stand…and suffer. But instead of being destroyed the church has flourished and grown by the millions. This is one of the *upside-down/opposite-world* ways that Christ uses to build His church and expand His kingdom. What the enemy seeks for destruction, God turns to life. And this should be our prayer as well.

Second, persecution is *unfounded*. No one should seek, encourage, or condone persecution. As I have said, it will find you. But neither should one run from persecution. It is a badge of honor, and the Lord will give you what you need at that time to stand firm in Him. But persecution is only blessed by God if it is unfounded: that is, not the just reward for wrongdoing, but for standing up for what is right ("for righteousness' sake," see 5:10). It should never be merely for some personal quirk or offense that we commit, but *because* we bear the name of Christ, we are persecuted ("falsely on My account," verse 11). As the apostle Peter expounds:

> Beloved, do not be surprised at the fiery trial when it comes upon you to test you, as though something strange were happening to you. But rejoice insofar as you share Christ's sufferings, that you may also rejoice and be glad when His glory is revealed. If you are insulted for the name of Christ, you are blessed, because the Spirit of glory and of God rests upon you. But let none of you suffer as a murderer or a thief

---

8 *Apologeticus*, Chapter 50. Quintus Septimius Florens Tertullianus (A.D. 160–220), early Christian author, apologist, and a polemicist against heresy. Tertullian has been called "the father of Latin Christianity."

or an evildoer or as a meddler. Yet if anyone suffers as a Christian, let him not be ashamed, but let him glorify God in that name (1 Pt 4:12-16).

AN INSTRUMENT OF THY PEACE

This, then, is the climax of paradox: happy...and *harassed*. Both the blessing on peacemaking and that on persecution assume an atmosphere of opposition: being thrown into situations where the peace has been broken, and called to make peace whole again; and thrown into places where persecution is certain, and called to be glad in it. It is a peculiar blessing—and a high calling. It is a calling that St. Francis understood well, as encoded in his classic prayer:

> Lord, make me an instrument of Thy peace: where there is hatred, let me sow love; where there is injury, pardon; where there is doubt, faith; where there is despair, hope; where there is darkness, light; and where there is sadness, joy. O Divine Master, grant that I may not so much seek to be consoled as to console, to be understood as to understand, to be loved as to love; for it is in giving that we receive, it is in pardoning that we are pardoned, and it is in dying that we are born to eternal life.

GOOD FOR THE WORLD

(Matthew 5:13-16)

You are the salt of the earth, but if salt has lost its taste,
how shall its saltiness be restored? It is no longer good for anything
except to be thrown out and trampled under people's feet.
You are the light of the world. A city set on a hill cannot be hidden.
Nor do people light a lamp and put it under a basket,
but on a stand, and it gives light to all in the house.
In the same way, let your light shine before others,
so that they may see your good works and
give glory to your Father who is in heaven.

IT is an all-too-common tendency in some conservative Christian circles to withdraw from the world into a "fortress mentality"; to step away from daily engagement with the world for fear of contamination by the world. This is often coupled with a mind-set of disregard for the improvement of the surrounding culture and society—like "polishing the brass on a sinking ship." There is no sense of urgency or even necessity to make any impact on the structures of the world, so we set up enclaves of protection from its corrupting influences. This instinct is not all bad; for certainly, we are to separate ourselves from the sins of the world and must protect especially the "little ones" from any occasions of stumbling (see Mt 18:6-7). As Christians, however, we can never separate ourselves from the world itself. It is a fundamental perspective: that rather than showing our disdain for the world, we should be showing our concern for the world.

For Jesus says, in no uncertain terms, that we are to be good for the world. The world (at every level) should be a better place because we are in it and because we are actively engaged with it. And He drives this point home by way of two metaphors: salt and light.

SALT OF THE EARTH

What is the meaning of this salt metaphor?[9] Salt functioned in the ancient world, as today, to enhance the flavor of food, but it also acted as a preservative, to delay decay. Before the age of refrigeration, it was a primary means of preserving meat. In both aspects, salt functions as an image of improvement. We are called "the salt of *the earth*" (5:13), which directly parallels "the light of *the world*" (verse 14). In other words, our presence on earth should make the world—as a whole and in all its parts—a better place.

It is no accident that these verses on living as salt and light are sandwiched between the Beatitudes and Jesus' examples of living out the Law (5:17-48). For when we truly live as followers of Christ, we will invariably improve our increasingly secularized and paganized society. For example, when we live out these individual character qualities found in the Beatitudes, we enhance whatever community we are involved in. Meekness discourages violence, mercy breeds mercy, humility thwarts selfishness, and peace makes for a kinder, safer society. Borrowing from Jesus' restatements of the Law: cutting off the roots of anger and lust will foster a culture of life and love (see Mt 5:22, 28), and discouraging divorce will stabilize the foundational unit of society—the family (Mt 5:31-32). To present a metaphor, the world should "taste better" because we are in it. Not only should we "enhance its flavor," we ought also to prevent "decay" in a moral sense. That is part of who we are and who we ought to be.

It seems a paradox to note the presence of so many churches—it sometimes seems there is one on every corner—and to see certain segments of our society saturated with a Christian presence, yet find that we are still dominated by societal ills that are completely contrary to the Christian vision. The gospel has not truly taken root if it does not govern our day-to-day decisions and interactions, if although supposedly redeemed in spirit, mind, and heart, we continue to live self-centered lives, apathetic toward the concerns and needs of others around us. Does the calling of

---

9 As R. T. France acknowledges: "The precise nature of the symbolism is not certain. The two most significant uses of salt in the ancient world were for flavoring and for the preservation of food, and either or both of those uses would provide an appropriate sense here." (The Gospel of Matthew, *The New International Commentary on the New Testament*, ed. Gordon D. Fee [Grand Rapids: William B. Eerdmans Publishing Company, 2007], 174).

kindness, for example, have any impact on how we drive, how we greet total strangers, or how we interact with our neighbors or co-workers? Do we treat others as we would want to be treated (the Golden Rule)? This is especially pertinent to how we treat our enemies or those who mistreat us. Do we lay down our lives for the good of the other person? How do we address issues of poverty on the one hand, or entitlement on the other? Are we governed by the mind-set of the world—or of the gospel? It is only when we refuse the one, and truly embrace the other—in other words, actuate our Gospel calling to be salt and light of the world—that we will see our communities, our culture, and our country transformed, even in small measures, by the beauty of Christ.

But in this metaphor, Jesus also introduces what is, on its face, a ludicrous question: "But if salt has lost its taste, how shall its saltiness be restored?" (5:13). Can salt lose its saltiness? The unadulterated chemical compound that we use today, sodium chloride, cannot. Most salt in the ancient world, however, such as the salt gathered around the Dead Sea, contained a mixture of impurities, the residue of which was cast away once the salt had been leached out.

But there is more going on here, it would seem. That the salt "has lost its taste" (verse 13) is literally, "has become foolish," (μωρανθῇ). This warns us of the folly and danger of conforming to the world rather than transforming it. Christians who compromise their Christianity for personal advantage or to avoid persecution or ridicule are in danger of being "thrown out" by God and, in the end, are still "trampled" by the world (5:13b). How often have we seen this happen within the church and with individual Christians who trade the approval of God for the applause of man, and end up with neither? Let us not be "fooled."

The apostle Paul picks up on Jesus' metaphor when he counsels the Colossian Christians:

> Walk in wisdom toward outsiders, making the best use of the time. Let your speech always be gracious, *seasoned with salt,* so that you may know how you ought to answer each person (Col 4:5-6).

Christians are to have a distinct influence for the better in society, perhaps because what we do and say is—or rightly ought to be—characterized by such wisdom and grace. If we do not strive to live our lives with wisdom and grace in what we do and say, then we are (in Jesus' words here) good for nothing, for we have not even grasped the basics of our calling—to be good for the world.

LIGHT OF THE WORLD

The second metaphor Jesus explores vis-à-vis our relationship to the world is that of light. But first let us step back a bit.

Light is our earliest and most fundamental need. Darkness we naturally abhor, even fear (particularly as children). For example, what is the one thing that keeps your children from being afraid to go to bed at night (other than scurrying into mom and dad's bed)? A bedside lamp. Or have you ever been lost or alone in the dark, in the woods? What is the one thing that calms your dread? A flashlight in hand or, better yet, one approaching in the distance. When the power goes out, what is the one thing that makes everything relatively all right? Simply, a candle lit. So we understand how darkness becomes symbolic of chaos and hopelessness, sin and death. It was darkness in the beginning, then God spoke, and there was light (see Gn 1:2-3). Light is what we naturally long for: light is life, light is hope, light is joy. So light naturally serves as an image of eternal life, of order, and of the hope and joy we so desperately need. It is an image of God's salvation.

In John 8:12, Jesus stood up and unequivocally declared: "*I* am the light of the world. Whoever follows Me will not walk in darkness, but will have the light of life." This bold statement was a direct fulfillment of several prophecies but, in particular, Isaiah 49:6, wherein God said:

> It is too light a thing that You should be My Servant
> to raise up the tribes of Jacob
> and to bring back the preserved of Israel;
> I will make You as a light for the nations,
> that My salvation may reach to the end of the earth.

This means that the world is in spiritual darkness, and Jesus alone is the light to lead us out of that darkness.

This theological statement stands in stark contrast with the spirit of the age—a spirit that teaches tolerance, relativism, and pluralism. The spirit of the age tells us that the truth of Christ is a truth for us alone rather than for the entire world, a truth that should be kept to ourselves rather than a truth to be shouted from the rooftops. The tolerance it professes is that Jews find their salvation in the Torah, Christians find their salvation in Christ, Muslims find their salvation in Allah, and that secularists have no need of salvation. Pluralism adds that Buddhists, Hindus, new agers, and neo-pagans all have their valid paths to "God." Indeed, there are some who declare that *all* paths are valid in that they all lead to the *same* God. But God Himself has spoken, and His verdict is Christ. He alone is the light of the world.

But that is not what Jesus is saying here. The astonishing thing is this: to all who are His disciples He says, "*You* are the light of the world" (5:14)! This is an incredible statement. Now, for this to be true, it must be Christ's light shining through us, for God has chosen to reveal His glory through us: the light of Christ "in jars of clay," as the apostle Paul describes it (2 Cor 4:7). If we shine the light of Christ, then we indeed become the light of the world. But who is it that the world in its darkness sees? Do they apprehend the genuine light of Jesus in our actions and in our words? Not perfection, by any means, but Christ. Do our lives and our lips point to Him, or are we merely an empty likeness, a hypocritical façade, a symbol without substance? Even the world in its darkness can discern the difference. What kind of light do you shine—wherever you are? This is the gospel imperative: that His light shines through us, in our words and deeds.

For this light to be legitimate, it must be visible. It must be publicly seen, not hidden from view. This speaks directly against the "fortress mentality" too common among Christians, or the tendency to withdraw from engagement with the world in so many spheres. Moreover, the pursuit of private piety—or the prevalent demand that we keep our piety separate from the public arena—does not fulfill this command: "let your light shine before others" (5:16). The old children's hymn says it so well:

> Jesus bids us shine with a clear, pure light,
>> Like a little candle burning in the night.
> In this world of darkness, we must shine:
>> You in your small corner, and I in mine.

And light is not unobtrusive. Light pierces the darkness, light dispels the darkness, light transforms the darkness. This is the forcefulness of Jesus' words when He says, "Nor do people light a lamp and put it under a basket, but on a stand, and it gives light to all in the house" (5:15). Thus the world, wherever you live, should be a brighter place because of your presence there.

Christ's light is seen in various "good works" (5:16)—that which we do in Jesus' name because we are His. In Matthew 25:35-36, which is a depiction of the judgment scene at the great Last Day, Jesus depicts these good works as feeding the hungry, clothing the poor, welcoming the stranger, and visiting the sick and the imprisoned. These are good works of compassion that shine especially bright and serve to authenticate the gospel as nothing else does. If you look throughout history, compassion ministries have always followed wherever the gospel goes. Why is that? Because serving the less fortunate is central to our Christian identity and our Christian calling. When the world sees this kind of light—not only the light of Christ in word, the glorious message of salvation, but also the light of Christ in deed, tangible acts of service to those in need—when they see us giving ourselves for the good of the world, they will indeed give glory to our heavenly Father.

What is our relationship, as Christians, to the world? That is a loaded question, certainly. But our Lord's description of His disciples as salt and light signifies something profound: that, fundamentally, we are to be *good* for the world. These are common, ordinary things, but they change everything for the better for all of mankind. Salt makes everything taste better (and many things last longer), and light brings with it both illumination and freedom. This is what we are to be in the world and for the world, to the glory of God. Are you bringing salt and light to your home? To your school or workplace? To your community and city? Even the whole world: Is it a better place because Christians are in it? Is our light and salt noticed by the non-Christians around us? Remember, Jesus tells us that if others observe our good works, they will glorify God (verse 16). If we are not living this way, then we need to do some serious self-examination and repent.

5

SAYS WHO?

(Matthew 5:17-20)

Do not think that I have come to abolish the Law or the Prophets;
I have not come to abolish them but to fulfill them.
For truly, I say to you, until heaven and earth pass away, not an iota,
not a dot, will pass from the Law until all is accomplished.
Therefore whoever relaxes one of the least of these commandments
and teaches others to do the same will be called least in the
kingdom of heaven, but whoever does them and teaches them
will be called great in the kingdom of heaven.
For I tell you, unless your righteousness exceeds that of the scribes
and Pharisees, you will never enter the kingdom of heaven.

IN the previous group of verses, Jesus addressed the relationship of the Christian and the world in terms of salt and light. These are common, ordinary things, but they change everything for the better. Jesus now addresses the relationship of the Christian and the Word—or as Jesus calls it here, the Law. This is an imposing word [10] at first; but Jesus is using it as just a way of referring to the will of God, the instructions of God, in the Bible. What does Jesus want us to understand about the Bible, and what does it mean for us?

ENDURING STANDARD

The first thing Jesus says about the Bible is that it is *an enduring standard.* This is something that is not often believed anymore. In our culture in

---

10 The basic sense of the Hebrew term for *law*, (תּוֹרָה transliterated, Torah), is this *instruction* from God. But law is also a revelation of the nature of things as God has created it. This applies to both the physical and spiritual realms; and there is a built-in correspondence between the two. Following God's law brings life and peace; violating God's law brings ruin and destruction. It is the natural consequence.

general, the Bible is considered passé—especially in regard to its moral pronouncements: most notably, in our society, those that speak to both homosexual and heterosexual practices. We are told that we live in a more enlightened and progressive and liberated age. The cry that constantly arises (and that we, sadly, too often accommodate or give in to) is that we need to adjust our standards to match the times. We may even believe that God needs to adjust His standards to match ours. So, it is a very important question: Is the standard relative, and is the Bible passé? Jesus says, "No."

But the Christian struggle is often much more subtle: the Bible is believed to be an enduring standard (in the abstract), but how really relevant is it (in the concrete)? Some may wonder what the stories of Old Testament Israel and her constant run-ins with God, or the lengthy regulations about animal sacrifices, have to do with us and our techno-modern lives. After all, we are sending people into space! Or what do the rules for Christian masters and slaves have to do with us in our free and democratic society? What relevance does any of this have to modern life? So we carefully pick and choose the "relevant" portions of Scripture to preach and teach and write books about: those things that at least seem to touch most clearly on our lives, and leave aside all the rest. We may tend to ignore most of God's Word and His revealed will for His people. And, so, the question is pertinent: Is the Bible relevant? Jesus says, "Yes." It may take some work, and faith, and humility to discover the riches of its relevance, but it is all there.

The people must have been wondering, especially after Jesus shared the Beatitudes where everything was turned upside-down, whether Jesus intended to set up a whole new system. Did Jesus come to abolish the Law and the Prophets (5:17)? To this, Jesus says, in no uncertain terms: "I have *not* come to abolish them, but to fulfill them." But then He says something equally startling: "Not an iota, not a dot [or, in the King James, "jot or tittle"], will pass from the Law" (5:18). Here Jesus is referring to the smallest letter in the alphabet, and the smallest mark that distinguishes one letter from another—in other words, including the smallest things that make up the very words in the Bible. The Bible, even to its minutiae, is trustworthy and will remain so until the end of time. It is truly an enduring standard. What does this mean for us?

First, it means that the Old Testament is part of our Bible. The Old Testament together with the New is our complete instruction manual—understood, of course, through the lens of Christ. Notice what part of the Bible Jesus is talking about here: the Law and the Prophets, that is, the Old Testament. Even the apostle Paul, in addressing the young pastor Timothy, was talking about the inspiration and edification of the Old Testament when he said that *"all* Scripture is breathed out by God and profitable" (2 Tm 3:16). But do we treat it that way? Or do we ignore it because it is old, or odd, or out of date?

Second, it means that the moral commands of God "remain." When God declares His will for us, this will does not evolve. Portions do not pass away as passé. God's word does not change with changing times. The Ten Commandments—and their various ramifications or amplifications that we see throughout Scripture—cannot be redefined to fit modern man's sense of tolerance or decency, nor can they be replaced by platitudes such as "if it feels good, do it, as long as it doesn't hurt anybody." We must take Scripture seriously. The Bible—in its entirety—is God's authority for my life. Who says so? Jesus does: "Truly, *I* say to you" (5:18).

IMPOSSIBLE STANDARD

The second thing Jesus says about the Bible is that *it sets an impossible standard*. If a typical American audience were asked, "How many of you want to go to heaven?" there would be a slew of hands raised. And if the questioner asked, "How many of you think you will get into heaven?" the number of hands would remain pretty high. Then if it were followed up with, "Why do you think *you* will get into heaven?" certainly many would say, "Because basically I'm a good person," or "I try to keep the Ten Commandments," or "I attempt to follow the Golden Rule." A great number of people would offer some version of these responses. But this is a common misunderstanding in our churches and culture today. This may be somewhat of a shocker—and it is meant to be: but access to heaven based upon our merit is absolutely *impossible* for us to attain. Says who? Jesus declares it so when He says: "For *I* tell you, unless your righteousness exceeds that of the scribes and Pharisees, you will never enter the kingdom of heaven" (5:20).

The scribes and Pharisees were the "righteous" people in Jesus' day.

They were the most righteous—in fact, they were meticulously righteous. Everyone knew it, and they were proud of it and confident in it. From an outside perspective, they were "squeaky clean." When it came to following the laws of God, they "crossed every *T* and dotted every *I*." They even put hedges around God's laws—additional laws for self protection—so that they would not even get close to disobeying the laws of God. A common example seen today in observant Judaism is this: God commanded us never to take His name in vain because it is most precious and should be revered. But to ensure that they would not ever take His name in vain, religious Jews developed *a system* by which they would never speak the name of God at all. That was not God's intent or desire. But, as far as *appearances* are concerned, it is very "religious" and "reverent" and "righteous."

Jesus did not argue with that. What He did say was something so much more severe that it shocks us. He did not say that they were not righteous; He said that they were not righteous enough! He said, "unless your righteousness *exceeds* that of the scribes and Pharisees, you will never enter. . ." (5:20).

And it gets worse. In fact, the part of Jesus' sermon dealing with the righteousness of God's law and its requirements on our hearts (5:17-48) is framed by the repetition of *impossible righteousness*, a righteousness that surpasses the most perfect people on the planet (5:20)—*and* a righteousness that matches even that of God Himself! "Be perfect, as your heavenly Father is perfect" (5:48). Nothing short of *perfection* is good enough!

So if *they* are not even good enough for God, then which of us has any chance at all? The answer is no one, because not one of us is perfect. If we seek to reach heaven by living a "good" life, we will never succeed. It is not that getting into heaven is difficult. It is that it is humanly impossible. For no one is capable of matching God's perfection; we all fall far short of His standard. As Romans 3:23 tells us, "All have sinned and fall short of the glory of God." If the glory of God is the standard—a glory that is reflected in His law—then none of us stands a chance—unless *God Himself* can make us righteous. This is what drives us to Jesus.

So this brings us back to the questions: What (or whom) are you trusting in for your eternal life? *Why* do you think *you will* get into heaven? Just how good does one have to be? The answers to these questions are what drive us to Jesus. This awareness is what propels us to the cross. It is the only way of getting to heaven, because on the cross, Jesus took our failings and wickedness upon Himself, and gave to us His righteousness! What a wonderful exchange (see 2 Cor 5:21). In the cross, our sins are washed away; we are made clean from the inside out! Now we are clothed in righteousness. But it is not *our* righteousness that we wear, it is His. And if we have the righteousness of Christ, then our righteousness indeed "exceeds that of the scribes and Pharisees" (5:20), all of God's grace, and nothing of my own.

CHRIST CENTERED, CHRIST FOCUSED

The third thing Jesus says about the Bible is that *it has its center and focus on Christ.* The key issue is in Jesus words: I have come "to *fulfill* them" (5:17). It is a simple statement, but its implications are huge. This is where Jesus sets our perspective on the Old Testament.

He did not come to set Himself up as a rival to the Old Testament. There is not a wrathful God in the Old and a merciful Christ in the New; there is not a salvation by works in the Old, and a salvation by grace in the New; it is not "bad Law" versus "good grace"—it is all the unfolding of God's grace to us in Christ. The Old and New Testaments are not rivals; they are two halves of the same Bible. "Jesus Christ is the same yesterday and today and forever" (Heb 13:8). Jesus does not dismiss any of the Old Testament, rather, He elevates and establishes it. And He does so by directing our attention to Him, for the Old Testament is centered and focused on Him.

We need to look for Him there. This is what Jesus Himself brought to our attention after His resurrection when "He opened their minds to understand the Scriptures," "beginning with Moses and all the Prophets, He interpreted to them in all the Scriptures the things concerning Himself" (Lk 24:45, 27). For all who have seen Jesus, the Old Testament will never be the same, because we will see it not as a dusty code for an ancient people, but as the living Word of God that reveals the wonders of His salvation in Christ.

As a basic statement—looking at the big picture, the whole canvas— what Jesus means is this: Everything in the Old Testament, indeed, in all the Scriptures, points *to* Him, propels us *toward* Him, is summed up *in* Him, and must be interpreted *through* Him.

In various ethical demands that Jesus addresses directly, we see a more explicit internalization and intensification of God's commands, such as, murder to anger and adultery to lust. It is the very transformation of the heart by the Holy Spirit that has always been God's goal for His people. This is revealed more clearly in Jesus; for He is the heart of God come down for us. As the apostle John tells us in his Gospel: Jesus, who "is in the bosom of the Father, has made Him known" (Jn 1:18).

Perhaps most notable is the sacrificial system in the Old Testament. Jesus did not abolish it, He fulfilled it, and that is why we no longer practice it. The same could be said of the Passover: an innocent lamb is killed, its blood spread on the top and sides of the door frame, and then all of the lamb is eaten so that its death is fully their own—with the promise that the judgment of God would not fall on them. Instead, He parted the sea itself to lead them out of bondage and into the blessings of the Promised Land. What a beautiful picture of what Jesus does for us! Consider the tabernacle worship: only the high priest with the blood of sacrifice could enter the holy presence; otherwise they would die by the sheer glory of that presence. Jesus is that temple, and by Him we enter into that glory.

This is all a picture pointing to the reality. It is like having a picture of a particularly beautiful spot you would love to visit—say, an ocean panorama. You look at that picture over and over, and dream about really being there. And then, one day, you pack your bags, hop a plane or take the car . . . and you are there! Standing in that majestic vista, do you then hold up your picture to look at? No! You happily set the picture aside in the sheer wonder of the moment: the vastness of the ocean and the crashing of its waves; the salt in the air and the wind in your hair; the "skee" of the gulls and the vastness of the sky. And this is what Jesus does: He opens our world and our understanding of God's Word to the wonders of His love.

So, What Is the Bible for Us?

First, the Bible is an enduring standard: all of it is God's Word for us. God's will does not change with our whimsy; it does not pass away as passé. It is always relevant for our lives, but we must search it out with a humble heart.

Second, the Bible sets an impossible standard: it sets a bar for heaven so high that no one is good enough to get in. The false god of our fancy is far too small and fickle. But as we begin to glimpse the awesome beauty and perfection of God's righteousness, the true God of the universe and eternity!—He is so beyond . . . that He must be the one to bring us in. And He does so by His grace: "For God so loved the world, that He gave His only Son, that whoever believes in Him should not perish but have eternal life" (Jn 3:16).

Third, the Bible has its center and focus on Christ: He is the fulfillment of all that has come before. He is the center of all God's saving activity. He is the focus of God's redemptive plan by which we may have an eternal relationship with Him. The message of the cross is what bridges and binds together our understanding of the whole Bible. Here is where God comes close to us, that we may come close to Him.

THE SPIRIT OF THE LAW

(Matthew 5:21-26)

You have heard that it was said to those of old,
"You shall not murder, and whoever murders will be liable to judgment."
But I say to you that everyone who is angry with his brother
will be liable to judgment;
whoever insults his brother will be liable to the council;
and whoever says, "You fool!" will be liable to the hell of fire.
So if you are offering your gift at the altar and there
remember that your brother has something against you,
leave your gift there before the altar and go.
First be reconciled to your brother, and then come and offer your gift.
Come to terms quickly with your accuser
while you are going with him to court,
lest your accuser hand you over to the judge,
and the judge to the guard, and you be put in prison.
Truly, I say to you, you will never get out
until you have paid the last penny.

I n this portion of Jesus' Sermon on the Mount, He begins to lay out several key examples of the righteousness that God desires and heaven demands (see Mt 5:20: a righteousness that exceeds that of the "good-est" people in the world, and thus that none of us can attain apart from Christ's work on the cross). He teaches us this by revealing to us the *spirit* of the law.

We are all used to hearing about the *letter* of the law and the *spirit* of the law. An old friend once related a personal story of what he calls "malicious obedience." On our nation's highways, the speed limit is clearly posted, and usually ranges from 55 to 70 miles per hour. One day, my friend was crossing the Golden Gate Bridge out of San Francisco, intentionally driving at precisely the posted limit for bridge traffic, 45 miles per hour. Needless to say, traffic began to crawl, with horns blaring and drivers furious. Soon, he heard the siren coming up behind him and a policeman pulled him over. "But officer, I was only going 45." The policeman countered, that his strict obedience to the letter of the law, by impeding the flow of traffic, had in fact violated the spirit of the law.

And so, as Jesus begins here by looking at one law in particular, murder, you might say, "the big one," the first on everyone's list of something that is *really* bad, He reveals for us the spirit of the law. But in so doing, He lays down two fundamental principles that apply to *all* of God's laws.

CUTTING AT THE ROOTS

THE FIRST PRINCIPLE is this: *God's laws are more difficult than they look.*

Look at the religious leaders, the scribes and Pharisees (5:20): they thought they had it made because they were impeccably righteous...on the outside. But not just them; let me ask each of *you:* How many of you have committed murder, none? So you say, "There, I'm safe. Put a check-mark next to that command; and I'm OK." This is how we tend to think, and they were no different. They thought that the laws of God were a list of *externals.* They thought that you could completely obey this command while at the same time hating, or holding a grudge, or calling each other names—just as long as no actual homicide was involved. But what Jesus issues is a resounding, "Not so." They would have also known this, if they had understood the nature of God's commands as they were given. What is the Tenth Commandment? "You shall not covet" (Ex 20:17). This is an *internal* issue. The list of God's *big ten* closes where all of them start: it closes at the level of the heart.

The commands of God are far deeper, and much more intrusive, than they might at first appear. "Don't murder? No problem." But as Jesus points out, the intent of God's laws reaches to the level of the heart. When the heart is exposed, none of us stands.

For example, few people like to pull weeds, but have to do it anyway. It is actually a very good spiritual lesson with many built-in teaching opportunities for our children. For unless you pull up the root, especially dandelions, for example, the weed will grow right back. The same with cutting down shrubs or trees—unless you cut out the roots, little shoots will start right back up. Jesus is digging and cutting at the roots of murder. What He reveals is something with which we all struggle, for the root of murder is anger (and insults). Who does not have a problem with *that?*

Anger issues are a huge problem in our society. Insults and put-downs are common—even tolerated. But Jesus says something horribly startling (in 5:21-22): just as the act of murder will justly send someone to hell, so also the underlying issues of the heart—that find expression in our words (Mt 12:36)—will also justly send us to hell, "for out of the abundance of the heart the mouth speaks," (Mt 12:34). This throws us again toward our Savior; for apart from Him we are without hope.

So, when we look at this law at the level of the heart, we see that the heart of murder is anger (5:22)—and so we are *all* murderers at heart! Now, the act of murder is not all that common among us; but anger is. Is there anyone here who has *not* gotten angry at somebody else (for something other than sin)? It is something we have to struggle with almost every day! But this is where murder starts; and this is what anger does: it kills. It breeds things like abuse, and abusiveness *kills,* divisiveness *kills,* resentment and bitterness *kill.*

A classic manifestation of that anger is in something so trivial as our verbal insults and name-calling (5:22). It is like yelling out, "You idiot!"—let alone the worse things we sometimes say (anyone guilty of that?). Murder is not all that common among us, but trading insults is. These words tear down and destroy. Our words have the power both of life *and death* (see Prv 18:21). The person who made up the ditty: "sticks and stones may break my bones, but words will never hurt me"—was just plain wrong.

"OK," you say, "I get the point. But how bad can it be? We all do it, and nobody gets killed—*literally.*"

Probably all would agree with the statement that Jesus quotes (5:21): that you should be sent to jail or even receive the death penalty for murder. Through judgment in man's civil courts, you would not be locked up or executed for being angry or throwing insults. But in *God's* court, even anger and insults will justly send us to hell and give us the death penalty; for God's heaven is holy, and all such things before God are sin, and "the wages of sin is death" (Rom 6:23).

This is huge because it means that even those little sins of the heart and mouth are enough to send each one of us to hell (5:22). "Just because I called someone a fool?" But remember this is Jesus talking—and not what we expect to hear from Him! He does not say, "As long as you try to be a good person, and don't do anything *really* bad." For again, if the standard is perfection (see 5:48), then none of us can make it; nobody stands a chance—without Jesus. This shows us both the gravity of our sin and the necessity of His grace. This is what we see displayed for us on the cross. For there, God "made Him to be sin who knew no sin, so that in Him we might become the righteousness of God" (2 Cor 5:21).

You might ask, however: "Is *all* anger sin, and akin to murder?" Good question. Part of the answer is understanding what Jesus is doing here in His "re-statements" of the law that are internalized and intensified. He is setting down the basic principles for us to grapple with and receive. But there are exceptions (or perhaps better, refinements) that we find. One of God's chief character traits is "slow to anger." Yet, in numerous places throughout the Scriptures, we see God expressing anger against such things as sin, injustice, and unbelief (that is *key*). Sometimes we see even Jesus Himself expressing this same strong emotion against such things as religious hypocrisy—because it harms lives and damns souls.

So, too, with us: we must desperately seek (by God's grace) to be "slow to anger"; and we must make sure that it is not selfish, but "righteous anger." Then we must also deal with it directly and appropriately—lest it overtake us (see Eph 4:26-27). All other anger, and the insults and abuse that follow, is sin and the heart of murder. This is "the big one." We have all broken it, and Jesus tackles it first head on.

TWO SIDES OF THE COIN

THE SECOND PRINCIPLE is this: *For every negative there is a positive.*

These are two sides of the same coin, or you could say, two ends of the same magnet. For every negative command to *avoid*, there is a positive one to *obey*. God's commands are not meant to be simply a series of: "do not do this, do not do that." Implied in each of them is its polar opposite, as Jesus Himself clarifies for us here. It is not enough to avoid actual homicide. We must also seek to protect and promote life and peace. The negative deals with death, so the positive must nurture life. This is what Jesus shows for us here, in the two examples that He follows up with (notice the start of verse 23: "So"; or "Therefore," NIV). They are illustrations of what it means to keep this command in the positive way.

Or, using the plant metaphor: There is a negative *root;* anger is the *root* of murder. But there is also a positive *fruit;* and peace is the *fruit* of obedience. So, when you look at this command from the top side of the soil: Are you seeking and doing things that nurture life? We have seen how anger kills and insults kill, but reconciliation and humility give life!

There are a couple of interesting things to notice about these two examples that Jesus gives. *The first point* is this: Although this first example deals with someone who is clearly a believer ("your brother," 5:23-24), the second deals with someone who is evidently not ("your accuser," 5:25-26). This illustrates the principle the Scriptures talk about elsewhere: If at all possible, live at peace with all people (see Rom 12:18). That is, not just your family, not just your buddies, not just your fellow Christians. Live at peace also with your non-Christian neighbors, or the kids you go to school with, or the people you work with, who might not be very nice or friendly people, who just might be tempted to take you to court if given the chance. Here Jesus tells us to seek peace.

Speaking of court, we live in a horribly litigious society, where suing is second nature, where even the most petty issues are brought before the courts and on TV. Why? To get satisfaction or to *show* the other person? But we are called to protect and promote life in relationships. We are called to peace. But real peace is not settled in the courts. The courts are there to decide and enforce big issues of justice; they cannot make peace. So, if there is a conflict between two people, we are to avoid the courts, if at all possible, and seek to settle things outside of that system—interpersonally—even if it means taking a loss. As the apostle Paul said regarding two Christians in court: "Why not rather be wronged" (1 Cor 6:7) than for the name of Christ to be shamed?

The second point is this: in both cases, the people Jesus calls us to seek peace with are not those who have wronged us or whom *we* think we have wronged. Rather, it is *they* who think that we have wronged them. The non-believer is *accusing* me and the believer *has something against me.* Should I care what other people think about my words and actions? *That is their problem.* Ultimately, before God, yes. But there is also a sense in which *I am* "my brother's keeper." I have to be concerned about whether something I do or say does wrong or causes harm to another. This is part of protecting and promoting life and peace—which is what it also means when God commands: "You shall not murder" (Ex 20:13).

But it goes deeper: we are not only called to care, we are called to seek out reconciliation. How many of our churches—and those within our churches—are ignoring this basic obedience? Does everyone love the fact that we have been reconciled to God? The Bible tells us that we were all alienated from God and hostile to Him, but that He embraced us into a relationship of friendship because of what Jesus did for us on the cross. He took away the cause of our enmity—sin (see Col 1:21-22). If God did this for us—before whom we gather to worship Sunday after Sunday—then how can we not strive to be reconciled with one another? This is a level of practical hypocrisy that we all too often live with, but that Jesus says cannot be. It is so important to Him that He even says it would be better to leave the altar and go to be reconciled with our brother first—and then come back. Then you will better understand who you are worshipping (5:23-24). Especially relevant is this when we come together around the Lord's Table: for this is the focus of "the altar," this is the place of our reconciliation. The altar that gives life calls us to seek life. The altar that gives peace also calls us to seek peace.

So then, what is the spirit of God's law? When God says, for example, "You shall not murder," He means not only the action itself, but also those attitudes of the heart, the desires and words, that express hurtful anger. When God says, "You shall not murder," He is not only preventing a negative, He is promoting a positive. He is promoting all those things that lead to life and peace with one another. This is what God desires; and this reveals how far we all fall short. This casts us all, if our hearts are not hard, onto the grace of God that He gives in Christ.

DEALING SERIOUSLY WITH SIN

(Matthew 5:27-30)

You have heard that it was said, "You shall not commit adultery."
But I say to you that everyone who looks at a woman with lustful
intent has already committed adultery with her in his heart.
If your right eye causes you to sin, tear it out and throw it away.
For it is better that you lose one of your members
than that your whole body be thrown into hell.
And if your right hand causes you to sin, cut it off and throw it away.
For it is better that you lose one of your members
than that your whole body go into hell.

HERE Jesus is addressing a very serious issue that has to do with our understanding of and attitude toward sin. He is looking at a particular sin again, but in a way that can apply to all of God's laws. In the previous verses, we saw Jesus bring out the *spirit* of God's laws, by looking at the law against murder. *Do not murder?* No problem, we think. But He showed us two things about the intent of God's righteous commands. (1) He showed us that God's laws are far harder than they look. They reach to the level of the heart, and the heart of murder is anger and insults. We all have a problem with that. In fact, the apostle John picks up on this when he explains that "everyone who hates his brother is a murderer" (1 Jn 3:15). And (2) God's laws are not just meant to forbid a negative; they are meant to promote a positive as well. They are two sides of the same coin. The flip-side of "do not murder" means that we must actively promote life and peace in relationships.

Here Jesus is looking at the command against adultery. All of you who are younger and unmarried may be thinking, "OK, I can skim through this one. I'm not even close to being married, so I can't possibly have to worry about adultery" (which by definition is sexual infidelity in a marriage covenant). Those of you who have been faithfully married for many years might have a similar reaction. But what Jesus does to this command as well is to apply it in such a way that it hits us all. There are two crucial truths we are to notice.

SERIOUS PROBLEM

TRUTH NUMBER ONE: the problem is serious. In fact, the problem of sexual sin is incredibly serious. Why? There are three chief reasons.

Powerful Drive

The first reason is because it is such a powerful drive. Our sexuality is like fire: mysterious and full of wonder, for one; but also, it has the tremendous potential for either good or evil, for blessing or destruction. Kept in its proper bounds, like a campfire, it provides warmth and light and calm, and cooks up a nice-smelling roasted meat dinner, too. But let it escape your control, say, a sudden gust of wind scatters some sparks on the nearby grass, and it can quickly spread into a wildfire, leaving nothing but charred destruction in its wake.

So it is with us. We are sexual beings—male and female: we were made that way. We were "wired" to bond (like protons and electrons). Ignoring that is ignoring nature. God created us with this "fire." He called it good and blessed it: "Be fruitful and multiply" (Gn 1:28). So, the desire is good, and the delight is good—when kept within God's design. But it is something that must be respected and protected. Otherwise, you are playing with fire. The writer of Proverbs (in 6:27), speaking of sexual immorality, used this same analogy: Can a man scoop fire into his lap and not be burned?

It is something very precious too. Our culture does not understand or proclaim this anymore. In our society (paradoxically), sex is everything and yet sex is nothing. It "sells" everything, yet it "means" nothing. Fornication is commonplace; pornography is everywhere. And what harm does it really do, you might be tempted to ask? But this is the most intimate relationship we have: to join body and soul. And so, abusing this intimacy does nothing but destroy. Even more, it is a glimpse of the relationship that God will share with us forever—the delights of heaven (see Eph 5:31-32;

and Rv 19:7), where heaven is the eternity of that moment in the marriage of the Lamb and His Bride.

So, it has great power—either for beauty or for desolation. Look at happily married couples, and you will see the beauty; look at those who have suffered sexual betrayal, and you will see the desolation.

Problem of the Heart

The second reason the problem is so serious is because it is a problem of the heart. Again, the outwardly righteous leaders that Jesus had referred to earlier (5:20) had come to believe that you could fully obey this command while at the same time nursing lust, fantasizing about another man's wife—just as long as no actual adultery was involved. This is just as if God was interested in *externals* alone! Do we not slip into this, too? As has often been said: *the heart of the matter is the matter of the heart.* And as Jesus shows us here, the heart of adultery is lust: *wanting someone who is not yours* (5:28).

This heart intent is nothing new. They should have known better, and we should know better. This is the seventh commandment, but three commandments down, God explicitly states (in Dt 5:21), "You shall not *covet* your neighbor's *wife*"! Both sin and righteousness start in the heart. The greatest commandment of them all begins, "You shall love the LORD your God with all your heart…" (Dt 6:5). James also describes how sin's progression starts:

> Each person is tempted when he is lured and enticed by his own
> desire. Then desire, when it has conceived, gives birth to sin;
> and sin, when it is fully grown, brings forth death (Jas 1:14-15).

So, just like the previous issue, murder, we might at first be tempted to say: "No adultery? No problem." But it is a huge problem, if it is in the heart; and that is where it is found in all of us, though men and women seem to wrestle with it in different ways.

No One Is Immune

The third reason the problem is so serious is because no one is immune. We all must pass through adolescence, with the blossoming of our sexuality and raging hormones. This prepares us for something beautiful; but it also presents us with an often intolerable struggle—for young men especially, and yet for us all. And marriage is no panacea. Just because you get married does not mean that you will no longer struggle with sexual temptation. During periods of marital discord or dissatisfaction, it becomes even more difficult, and the devil knows it, and will seek to exploit it. This leads many to look elsewhere—either for comfort or excitement.

And then there is the 600-pound gorilla in the middle of the room: pornography. The church is not immune from this either. A 2006 poll conducted by ChristiaNet.com[11] revealed that, from the 1,000 people who responded, 50 percent of those Christian men were addicted to pornography; and, perhaps surprisingly, 60 percent of Christian women who responded had significant struggles with lust! With the advent of high-speed internet, this has become an increasingly serious problem.

SERIOUS SOLUTION

If the problem is serious, then there is **TRUTH NUMBER TWO**: the solution must be equally serious. It requires radical obedience, and this is what our Lord calls us to (5:29-30). There are three principles to keep in mind.

Understand that Sin Destroys

THE FIRST PRINCIPLE is this: we need to understand the severity of the issue. This is not one of those "take two aspirin and call me in the morning" things. Personal sin is not to be coddled, accommodated, or handled with kid gloves. Jesus uses the harsh language of self-mutilation and amputation. Someone else has drastically called this: "chain saw repentance"! But you get the point: when you have serious sin issues, you do not pick up the scalpel, you pull out the chain saw.

This is part of understanding the nature and destructiveness of sin. Yes, sin has its pleasure…for a season. But in the end, sin always destroys, and it destroys mercilessly. It destroys what is most precious to us. This is one reason, in addition to the fact that I love them and they are dear to me, that I keep pictures of my wife and kids around as a tangible reminder, that if I sinned in this way—that would *destroy* them *from* me. As the writer of Proverbs warns:

---

11 http://christiannews.christianet.com/1154951956.htm

> The lips of a forbidden woman drip honey,
> and her speech is smoother than oil,
> but in the end she is bitter as wormwood,
> sharp as a two-edged sword.
> Her feet go down to death
> (Prv 5:3-5).

When you are tempted toward sexual immorality, think: "but do I want . . . death"!

A couple of other observations. Jesus mentions the right eye and the right hand. But why does Jesus attack them? One reason is because the eyes (seeing) and hands (doing) are two of primary offenders in sexual sin. And in most cases and in ancient thought, the right member was considered the most important, as the strongest and most frequently used. Just try writing or eating with your left hand (if you are right-handed), and you get the point. But if what you rely on is causing you to fall into sin, then it has got to go. It would be better (for example) not to have TV or the internet at all, or not to have that job that mandates excessive travel, if it is the occasion for destruction.

Also, although Jesus is speaking very graphically, He is not speaking literally. We are not to follow the example of the early church father, Origen, who, in the zeal of his youth, castrated himself. This is taking literally what is obviously a figure of speech. It does not solve the inner problem addressed. For a blind and crippled man can still lust just as easily, since it is in the heart.

Take the Necessary Steps

THE SECOND PRINCIPLE is: we must take whatever steps are necessary. To root out sin, radical measures must be taken. Martin Luther once said: "You can't keep the birds from flying over your head; but you *can* keep them from making a nest in your hair." So, how do I keep the birds of lust from building a nest in my heart and life? There are five steps, which I have labeled with five "R's."

FIRST—*Recognition*:

We need to begin by recognizing our own frailty and susceptibility. Do not flirt with sin, or pretend you are strong enough, or that it will not destroy you or the relationships you hold most dear. Just ask King David, the "man after God's own heart" (1 Sm 13:14).

SECOND—*Replacement:*

There are different approaches to this aspect, but the same basic idea. Some call it "bouncing eyes." Others would say, "Yes, Lord, you made her beautiful, but she is not mine." Another tactic is to pray, "Count your blessings. Thank you, Lord, for the spouse you have given me." Coupled with this is the need to feed the mind and heart with things that are good and godly, instead of things that are impure (Phil 4:8). Consider this story: An old Cherokee Indian was talking to his grandson about the struggle that goes on inside each of us: "It is like two wolves fighting inside us: one is evil—it is anger, greed, pride; the other is good—kindness, generosity, humility." The grandson thought for a while, and then asked: "Which wolf wins in the end?" The old man simply replied: "The one you feed."

THIRD—*Reinforcements:*

When the military or police find themselves in a situation that is over their heads, they call for reinforcements to keep them from being blown to bits. How many Christian families have been blown to bits by sexual sin? So too, knowing our weaknesses, we need to set up safeguards to keep us from falling. Perhaps it might be an accountability partner, or only using the computer in public areas. As a pastor, for protection of both parties, I make it a practice not to counsel with a woman unless there is another person nearby. From another angle: Christian women, you are your "brother's keeper" and we are to help each other. So then, knowingly dressing and acting in such a way that naturally entices a man other than your husband to lust is not "loving your neighbor as yourself."

FOURTH—*Run:*

The Scriptures show us that we have three main enemies: the world, the flesh, and the devil. Just like warfare, different enemies demand different tactics. We are to fight (resist) the devil[12]; we are to flee the flesh. If we get those turned around, we will only invite defeat. If we flee the devil, he will tear us up from behind. If we fight the flesh, we will fall. This is what Joseph understood (Gn 39), when propositioned by Potiphar's

---

12 For this imagery, see Ephesians 6:11-17. See also James 4:7, and 1 Pt 5:8-9.

wife. She was beautiful, seductive, persistent…and no one would ever know. But God knew, and she was not his. If he stayed, he would fall; remember, that is how we are naturally wired. So, Joseph ran. He suffered in the short run, but God blessed him in the long run. Also, we must run in two directions. As the apostle Paul counseled young pastor Timothy, there must be both a *running from* and a *running to* (2 Tm 2:22):

> *Flee* youthful passions, and *pursue* righteousness, faith, love, and peace, along with those who call on the Lord from a pure heart.

FIFTH—*Repentance:*

This should be our daily attitude: we must turn *from* our sin and *to* God. We must constantly return to the cross and to Jesus, relying upon His grace and the power of the Spirit.

Always Remember Grace

This leads us to THE THIRD PRINCIPLE: always remember there is *grace*. Without this, we might be tempted to just give up and give in, for otherwise, it is impossible. Indeed, the *problem* and the *solution* are so serious *to God* that He sent His only beloved Son to the cross—for you and me. And because of this, we have the wonderful promise: that "if we confess our sins, He is faithful and just to forgive us our sins and to cleanse us from all unrighteousness" (1 Jn 1:9)—even if we come to Him over and over again (recall the "seventy times seven" in Mt 18:22). And because of this open welcome and grace, Jesus gives us hope, Jesus gives us liberty, Jesus gives us life!

MY FIGHT

As we have seen, God's command against adultery is not just for married heterosexuals. It is for us all. For the heart of adultery is lust, and lust is an equal opportunity *destroyer,* one that is not to be trifled with. The problem is serious; the solution must be equally serious. Praise the Lord that *He* took the problem and the solution so seriously in the cross. For it is through His cross that we can daily find cleansing, renewal, and victory. Let me close with a poem I composed when I was making my own transition into adulthood, and fighting this very issue:

My adversary faces me, a vision of my self;
A shadowed, dark reflection filled with blunt, seducing stealth.
We draw our weapons—one must win this fight to gain the ground
Of battles fought, and future still, yet all without a sound.
The place: an inward pedestal, the feature of the mind;
The struggle: ever present—one must win, and one must die.
We circle 'round, my dim self strikes, I block the blow with might;
We stand locked for a moment in the pressure of the fight....
Yet, when the sweat began to form, I gazed into his eyes,
And saw there all my selfishness, my lust, my greed, my lies.
My grip began to weaken for I saw my false desire;
My shadow reason beckoned me, and I began to tire.
My inward voice cried, "Run away! This thing you cannot fight!"
I stayed and sank down to my knees, and felt the wicked bite.
"I won! I won!" my self proclaimed. My inward voice now swore:
"Oh, you have won this battle, yes, but I shall win the war."

WHAT GOD
HAS JOINED TOGETHER

(Matthew 5:31-32)

It was also said, "Whoever divorces his wife,
let him give her a certificate of divorce."
But I say to you that everyone who divorces his wife,
except on the ground of sexual immorality,
makes her commit adultery, and whoever marries
a divorced woman commits adultery.

W HEN you look at the divorce rate in our nation (and the church is sadly keeping track with this decline), we see that it used to be that divorce was sought and granted for "real" reasons—like adultery or abuse. Beginning in 1970 with the advent of "no-fault" divorce laws, now in all but one of the 50 states,[13] you can break a marriage contract as easily as, or in many cases, easier *than* any other contract, and for something as nebulous as the characteristic "irreconcilable differences," which can cover just about anything. And so we now rationalize and legislate ways to make it easier to separate what God has joined together—violating the fundamental principle Jesus expresses later on in this Gospel (Mt 19:6). This is now the way of the world, and sadly, it has become the way of the church as well. But we are called to something radically different and tremendously better. I remember when I was a teenager, two prominent Christian leaders, whom I had up until that time respected, both proclaimed that they were divorcing their Christian spouse...for the sake of the ministry!

---

13 New York remains the only state in the union that technically does not allow for a no-fault divorce.

Well, it was not really any different back then, either. The institutional "church" in Jesus' day, that is the Jewish religious leadership, also typically led the church and society in trivializing the covenant of marriage. Jesus faces this travesty head-on, and He states in no uncertain terms: this must not be so.

THE CART BEFORE THE HORSE

In His opening statement (5:31), Jesus refers back to the teaching found in Deuteronomy 24:1-4, and the way that text was freely used as the justification and grounds for divorce.

> When a man takes a wife and marries her, if then she finds no favor in his eyes because he has found some indecency in her, and he writes her a certificate of divorce and puts it in her hand and sends her out of his house, and she departs out of his house, and if she goes and becomes another man's wife, and the latter man hates her and writes her a certificate of divorce and puts it in her hand and sends her out of his house, or if the latter man dies, who took her to be his wife, then her former husband, who sent her away, may not take her again to be his wife, after she has been defiled, for that is an abomination before the LORD (Dt 24:1-4).

When Jesus is confronted by the Pharisees on this very issue and text once again in Matthew 19, we see explicitly how they were putting the cart before the horse. They ask (in Mt 19:3): "Is it lawful to divorce one's wife *for any cause?*" (they were certainly champions of "no-fault divorce"). They were putting the exception before the rule—wanting to know just how *wide* were the bounds for legitimate divorce. But this mind-set is completely wrongheaded, and Jesus seeks, in a simple but forceful response, to redirect us to God's perspective, which is keeping the horse far out in front.

In the time of Jesus, there were two basic schools of thought with regard to divorce—both based on the teaching found in Deuteronomy 24:1. The Oral Law (those binding traditions of the scribes and Pharisees encoded in the Mishnah—and that Jesus often butted heads with) describes the debate, stemming from this verse:

> The House of Shammai say, "A man should divorce his wife only because he has found grounds for it in unchastity, since it is said, *Because he has found in her indecency in anything.*" And the House of Hillel say, "Even if she spoiled his dish, since it is said, *Because he has found in her indecency in anything.*" R. Aqiba says, "Even if he found someone else prettier than she[!], since it is said, *And it shall be if she find no favor in his eyes*" (*Gittin* 9:10).[14]

As you can see, Shammai emphasized the "indecency" part (specifically, sexual); Hillel the "anything." And as you can imagine, the liberal Hillel position was much more popular with the men, since it was the men alone who could issue a divorce—and it gave them pretty much a "blank check."

But although Jesus is much closer to the Shammai side, He is actually much stronger than both. For both of them were legislating out of the problem; Jesus wants to legislate from the principle, from God's design, from what marriage itself was intended to be. Borrowing from His later answer to this very issue, His point is simply what we find stated at the close of so many wedding ceremonies: "What therefore God has joined together, let not man separate" (Mt 19:6). "One flesh" is not to be divided. This is the marriage principle; this is God's intent. And we need to weigh that heavily in our minds before we get distracted by "irreconcilable differences," or a laundry list of grievances, or falling out of love, or becoming tempted to take the easy way out and just throw in the towel.

Besides, if we understand marriage properly, we are to see that there is something tremendously profound that is going on here. Marriage between a man and wife is not just some social contract of convenience, companionship, progeny, or pleasure. It is a living picture of the relationship between Christ and His church—an indissoluble bond of honor and love.

> "Therefore a man shall leave his father and mother and hold fast to his wife, and the two shall become one flesh." This mystery is profound, and I am saying that it refers to Christ and the church. However, let each one of you love his wife

---

14 Jacob Neusner, *The Mishnah: A New Translation* (New Haven, CT: Yale University Press, 1988), 487 (emphasis added).

as himself, and let the wife see that she respects her husband (Eph 5:31-33).

We need to seek to live this out, even in our difficulties that we all go through in this fallen earth with our many sins. We should seek to live out this relationship for all to see. They should see that your spouse is always esteemed in a meaningful way in your eyes, and whenever there is conflict there is also the impulse to reconcile. One of the closing pictures of heaven strikingly portrays the church joining with the Lamb as His Bride (Rv 19:7), and heaven itself is the place of celebration of that union. Let us seek to taste and show some of that even now.

THE QUESTION OF DIVORCE

More and more, however, we are getting away from this sense, and even heaping abuse upon it. An egregious example has recently come out of Florida. Tony Perkins of the Family Research Counsel commented in a post late in 2007:

> In one Florida region, ending your marriage could be just a few mouse clicks away. The *Sun Sentinel* is reporting that the Broward County Clerk of Courts is now allowing residents to file for divorce online—"without leaving the house." ... The "self-service system," which sounds more like a supermarket check-out line than a way to break couples' vows, is "intended for people who can not afford an attorney or do not want to spend money on one." Besides, [Kris] Mazzeo [of the county court] says, "People come downtown, and it's expensive to park. If we can keep them from making extra trips to the courthouse, it would be great for them." That's outrageous! Are local officials more concerned about the price of parking than they are about the social costs of divorce? These Florida counties have it completely backward. We should not be making it easier for people to dissolve their marriages—we should be making it harder for them to overlook the resources to save their marriages. Decisions like this only serve to cheapen a sacred institution and belittle divorce's toll on families and children.

So too, in this as in all things, we should not be looking at our marriages and asking what the boundaries are for getting *out*, but what it is intended to be in the first place—and work *from* that, and work *for* that. Divorce is never this "good" thing as society often touts it; it is always the result of sin and failure. It may be the preferable option in the face of such things as repeated adultery and abuse, like "the lesser of two evils," but it is by no means the ideal path to choose. It is the path of last resort—and only when the covenant itself has already been breached. Even this regulation under Moses that Jesus refers to was given as a protection *for* the divorced wife, not as some sanction for divorce itself.

But, in our realism, the question still haunts us: "Is divorce and is remarriage ever okay?" And Jesus says, in one case, "Yes." In our fallen world, the horse still does pull a cart—but it is a very small cart. The only exception Jesus allows for here is "sexual immorality" (5:32). In that case, the marriage union has already been broken by the forming of a new "one flesh" relationship. But even this does not make divorce necessary, only legitimate, because with genuine repentance, wonderful things can happen. Broken hearts and homes can be healed.

But what about extreme situations—not just adultery, but abandonment or abuse? By Jesus' own admission of an exception for infidelity, He lets us know that there are indeed exceptions to the rule: but they are just that—exceptions, so much so, that they can even go without being mentioned or allowed at all (see Mk 10:11-12). The apostle Paul brings one out in 1 Corinthians 7:15—that of willful desertion by an unbelieving spouse. All such matters must be weighed with special care and wisdom, through precautionary steps taken to avoid divorce such as temporary separation, godly counsel, and opportunity for tested repentance and reconciliation. But we, like them, have made the exceptions the rule and largely ignored God's intent. If the standard, in Christian circles, is that marriage is one man and one woman for life, we need to start living it! Of course, it is not easy. But the Lord gives the ability, and the Lord blesses.

God's design for our marriage is permanence. God's intent for our marriage is fidelity. These are indeed "holy bonds of matrimony." Jesus drives home His point, that breaking these bonds is sin. For Jesus, it is as simple as that. Let us come back and truly hear His words.

YOUR WORD IS YOUR BOND

(Matthew 5:33-37)

Again you have heard that it was said to those of old,
"You shall not swear falsely,
but shall perform to the Lord what you have sworn."
But I say to you, Do not take an oath at all, either by heaven,
for it is the throne of God, or by the earth, for it is His footstool,
or by Jerusalem, for it is the city of the great King.
And do not take an oath by your head,
for you cannot make one hair white or black.
Let what you say be simply "Yes" or "No";
anything more than this comes from evil.

JESUS is the breaker of bonds. He came to proclaim freedom for prisoners from the bondage of sin, the power of Satan, and the constraints of the world (see Lk 4:18). Yet, at the same time, we who bear the name of Christ bear the bonds of Christ. We have been set free from our bondage to sin, but we have become slaves of God (Rom 6:22).

In these verses, and in the immediately preceding ones, Jesus confronts us with what we ought to consider as two unbreakable bonds: the bond of marriage, and the bond of our word. To do so is to run counter to the culture—both for our day as well as for His, amongst the religious establishment as well as the secular. Yet, the significance of these two bonds runs deeper than the bonds themselves, for they picture profound spiritual realities.

In marriage (as we saw in the last chapter), we image the relationship of Christ and His church. With our word, we image God whose word is truth, whose word is sure, and whose word gives life (see Gn 1; Jn 1).

THE APPARENT CONTRADICTION

The particular question that Jesus addresses with regard to our words is this: Is it ever appropriate to utter an oath? His categorical statement here: "Do not take an oath at all" (5:34) and His sobering conclusion: "anything more than this comes from evil" (5:37) seem to issue a resounding "No!" It is never appropriate as a follower of Christ to issue an oath of any kind.

This is certainly strong and unqualified language. And because of this, some Christian groups, such as Quakers and Mennonites, typically refuse to say the "Pledge of Allegiance" or to take the oath in court: "Do you swear to tell the truth, the whole truth, and nothing but the truth, so help you God?" And James echoes this same strong language:

> But above all, my brothers, do not swear, either by heaven or by earth or by any other oath, but let your "yes" be yes and your "no" be no, so that you may not fall under condemnation (5:12).

This is clearly an echo of Jesus' own exhortation, and clearly straightforward and direct.

But His words seem to stand in direct contradiction to the teaching of the Old Testament, although even here, we must remember His opening salvo, "I have not come to abolish them but to fulfill them," (5:17). So we read in the Scriptures that God Himself *commanded* oaths to be taken in His name: "You shall fear the LORD your God. You shall serve Him and hold fast to Him, *and by His name you shall swear*" (Dt 10:20). And God even took them in certain solemn and significant cases: "The LORD swore to David a sure oath from which He will not turn back" (Ps 132:11). With regard to the Abrahamic promise, the author of Hebrews writes:

> For people swear by something greater than themselves, and in all their disputes an oath is final for confirmation. So when God desired to show more convincingly to the heirs of the promise the unchangeable character of His purpose, He guaranteed it with an oath (Heb 6:16-17).

So, the oath—in and of itself—cannot be "from evil," as Jesus bluntly stated, without impugning God's character, without assigning evil to God

(God forbid!). Even Jesus Himself answered while under oath at court (Mt 26:63-64).

So, it would appear that for the conscientious follower of Christ, there is a legitimate place and time for an appropriate oath as something especially solemn, significant, and public, that you can look back on with a particular gravity. This is especially pertinent to official oaths that others ask of us for legal or covenant purposes, for instance: the oath one takes before testifying in court, or the wedding vows that are spoken "before God and these witnesses." It is highly unlikely (given the larger Biblical context) that Jesus meant to utterly repudiate these.

But the issue here is properly not on the merits of oath-taking, but the importance of truthfulness: the absolute necessity of honesty. Jesus, as is His custom, states matters here categorically—as in His calls to discipleship: for example, hate everyone, sell everything (Lk 14:26; 18:22). He does so in order to drive home His point: that our word is our bond, and anything that takes away from this fundamental integrity is coming completely from the wrong side.

THE HEART OF THE MATTER

Like the other matters in this portion of His sermon, Jesus is addressing the issue of misuse and abuse.

The people of His day had made the issue of keeping their word dependent upon how it was worded—how closely their oath was related to God. The closer it was, the more binding the oath; otherwise, you did not *necessarily* have to keep it. In fact, the Mishnah (mentioned before) has an entire tractate on oaths. And one verse details how, if you swear an oath by God, then you are liable; but if you swear by heaven and earth, then you are exempt (*Shabuot* 4:13[15]; see also Mt 23:16-22). This is the very kind of thing that Jesus was addressing here, and the very kind of thing that He was seeking to counter: wiggling out of our responsibility to integrity, using our words to personal advantage rather than simply speaking "the truth, the whole truth, and nothing but the truth"—and holding ourselves accountable to it. Indeed, our Lord's response stands in direct objection to this tendency to "swear falsely"—even under a religious

---

15 Jacob Neusner, *The Mishnah: A New Translation* (New Haven, CT: Yale University Press, 1988), 629.

façade; to get out from under the obligation that my word is my bond.

Similarly, we have all heard the notorious "spin" on broken presidential promises under former president Clinton, although he did not have the monopoly on such a fault: "He kept all the promises he *intended* to keep"! And in our own experience, it is usually the liars and the untrustworthy who take refuge in pleading, "I swear!" in order to get us to believe what they say. With a dishonest person, this is no greater guarantee, regardless of the strength of the promise. This is just plain "evil," as our Lord calls it. Rather, our daily conversation and reputation ought to be such that our simple word is good. A simple "yes" or "no" should be all that is needed to guarantee what we say.

"You are only as good as your word" and "your word is your bond." We used to have statements like this that we lived by, and for Christians especially, we need to recapture this distinct and distinctive sense of integrity. For if we cannot stand by our simple word—a word that is to mimic God's own word: that what He says, He performs—then we have failed to image Him at a most basic level.

The measure of a Christian's word is truth. It is consistent and dependable. In fact, it is this that so clearly marks his testimony. As the psalmist David relates:

> O LORD, who shall sojourn in Your tent?
> Who shall dwell on Your holy hill?
> He who walks blamelessly and does what is right
> *and speaks truth in his heart...*
> who swears to his own hurt and does not change
> (Ps 15:1-2, 4).

or as the NIV renders this last phrase:

> who keeps his oath even when it hurts.

As we have already seen (notably, in 5:29-30), Jesus often makes use of hyperbole—overstatement—to cut to the heart of the issue. The particular issue that Jesus wrestles with here (various permutations on oath-taking) might seem a bit foreign to our everyday experience, but we must not let this detract from the weight of what he is saying to us. Jesus insists that God's intent for our words is honesty and integrity. Anything that detracts from that is just evil. For Jesus, it is as simple as that.

WHAT IS WRONG WITH
MY RIGHTS?

(Matthew 5:38-42)

You have heard that it was said, "An eye for an eye and a tooth for a tooth."
But I say to you, Do not resist the one who is evil.
But if anyone slaps you on the right cheek, turn to him the other also.
And if anyone would sue you and take your tunic,
let him have your cloak as well.
And if anyone forces you to go one mile, go with him two miles.
Give to the one who begs from you,
and do not refuse the one who would borrow from you.

As Americans, we live in a "rights" society. Our nation was founded on rights—good rights. We have even got a Bill of Rights that enumerates such Biblical liberties as association, worship, speech, travel, and the press. These are all good and precious things, and they are there to protect not only my own rights, but also the rights of others, in order to secure "liberty and justice for all."[16] In fact, to the Founding Fathers, these human rights were simply an expression of "what is right" in accordance with the laws of God.[17] So, the basic system of American rights is a beautiful (though partial and imperfect) reflection of God's revealed will. They reflect not only the spirit of Matthew 5, but also the protections implied in the Ten Commandments (distilled in the two great commands: love God, love each other).

---

16 Therefore, the signers of the Declaration of Independence were ready to sacrifice "their lives, their fortunes, and their sacred honor" in order to secure these rights, this pledge of freedom and justice, for everyone else.

17 Of notable mention are the repeated calls for societal justice so common in the prophets. See, for example, Isaiah 1:16-17; 58:1-12; 59:1-15; Jeremiah 21:12–22:17; Hosea 10:12-13; Amos 5:21-24.

However, this Biblical foundation of rights has devolved in our society into a basically selfish attitude that we each have the right to have things our own way. Rather than approaching life thankful for the many privileges we possess, we grumble about what we think we should get. (Does this remind you of the Israelites in the wilderness?) But as Christians this kind of rights-mentality is all wrong. So, what is wrong with wanting my rights? It is wrong when it becomes focused on "self" rather than on what is truly right.

But also, as humans, we live with a "retaliation" instinct. If somebody hits us, what is our natural reaction? We want to hit him back—and harder. Or if somebody calls you a horrible name, what is your instinct? To call him a name that hurts just as badly—or worse. You see, we are born with an instinct for retaliation. It is part of our sinful nature. It is one way we know that we are sinners. It is evil and it happens so fast, naturally, and from the heart. If someone hurts us, we *want* to hurt him back, and worse, if possible. We want payback, we want tit-for-tat, we want to get even. There are numerous examples of this regularly on the news. One example came out of Charleston, South Carolina, a couple of years ago. There were two city councilmen who did not get along. One of them had parked his car in the slot reserved for the other. So what did the wronged man do? He nonchalantly walked behind the other councilman's car and "keyed" along the rear end of his vehicle. One problem, it was caught on videotape. We look at this man with shame and well we should. But this is a deep issue in each of us, is it not? This is what our Lord addresses for us here: first, by looking at what is *wrong*, and then second, by looking at what is *right* and turning each of them on their head. It is *wrong* to exert the "right" of private retaliation. It is *right* to endure the wrong of personal injustice.

EXERTING MY RIGHT

FIRST, Jesus shows us what is *wrong*: to exert any so-called "right" of private retaliation. This supposed right is just plain wrong.

Jesus opens with His formulaic, "You have heard that it was said, 'An eye for an eye and a tooth for a tooth'" (5:38). And He is quoting here what has been called in common parlance the *lex talionis*: the "law of retaliation." At one level, this sounds great to us; but at another, it is repulsive.

We tend to like the part that sees a justification for pay-back: "Do unto others what they have done unto you." Again, this is our instinct, but it is wrong. It is wrong, partly because it has been twisted from its intent—as even the religious leaders back then had done. They believed, as we can infer by what follows, that if someone slapped you on the cheek, you had the God-given right to slap that man back: "a slap for a slap."[18]

Because we have been raised in a Christian context and informed by a Christian conscience, this very "tit-for-tat" part seems repulsive to us. Where is the mercy? "Eye for an eye"—it sounds so cold to us. "Law of retaliation"—it sounds like a horrible law. Again, it is repulsive, and rightly so, because it has been twisted.

So, let us look into this *lex talionis*, this "eye for an eye," as it was laid down from the beginning.

THE FIRST THING we need to see is that this is *God's* law. Now, this might shock us at first, but this law was laid down by God Himself—not some mere human, fallible and prone to sin. He said it, not just once, but three times in the Old Testament: in Exodus 21, Leviticus 24, and Deuteronomy 19! Yet, it looks as though Jesus is overthrowing this principle, is He not? So, has God's righteousness changed? But as Jesus Himself introduced this section of His sermon: "I have *not* come to abolish" the Law (Mt 5:17).

THE SECOND THING we need to notice is that this is God's law *of justice.* In the Old Testament, this law was given not in a personal but in a judicial context—the context of the courts. Deuteronomy makes this the most clear:

> A single witness shall not suffice against a person for any crime or for any wrong in connection with any offense that he has committed. Only on the evidence of two witnesses or of three witnesses shall a charge be established. If a malicious witness arises to accuse a person of wrongdoing, then both parties to the dispute shall appear before the LORD,

---

18 This instinctive reaction, that Jesus seeks to forestall, is markedly different than the justified—even Biblically necessary—reactions of self-defense in the face of egregious harm or the defense of others who are facing egregious harm. It is a standing Biblical mandate that we are to protect and preserve human life; and in particular, that we are to come to the defense of the helpless (see, for example, Psalm 82:2-4; Proverbs 31:8-9; Jeremiah 5:28-29).

before the priests and the judges who are in office in those days. The judges shall inquire diligently, and if the witness is a false witness and has accused his brother falsely, then you shall do to him as he had meant to do to his brother. So you shall purge the evil from your midst. And the rest shall hear and fear, and shall never again commit any such evil among you. Your eye shall not pity. It shall be life for life, eye for eye, tooth for tooth, hand for hand, foot for foot (Dt 19:15-21).

This "eye for an eye," then, does not justify the right for revenge. The Scriptures are not to be understood in this way. In fact, the Old Testament warns us against this very thing:

Do not say, "I will do to him as he has done to me;
I will pay the man back for what he has done" (Prv 24:29).

Rather, this divine principle was designed to ensure justice: *that the punishment would indeed fit the crime*—not over-punish nor under-punish. Their tendency, in those days, was to over-punish; our tendency, in the present day, is to under-punish. But what God is concerned about in society is *justice*. This law establishes that, in very concrete terms. Even in the Old Testament, however, we see that this could be broadly applied. For example, if you broke a slave's tooth, the slave went free (Ex 21:27). And it is on this very principle that any civilized judicial system is established.

This leads us to THE THIRD THING, and that is: God has different rules for society and for Christians, and we go astray when we mix these up. The rule for society is "justice." The rule for Christians, however, is "love." The apostle Paul talks about this very distinction in Romans 12 and 13. There, the duty of the state is to repay evil and reward good (see Rom 13:3-4), however, we are called to "repay no one evil for evil...but overcome evil with good" (Rom 12:17, 21).

This does not mean that individual Christians are to remain aloof from matters of justice, for justice is part of our calling.[19] But it is not our first governing principle—love is.[20] However, there is a clear distinction

---

19 See, for example, Micah 6:8.
20 See, for example, Matthew 22:36-40.

in the Scriptures between defending oneself and others from genuine harm or death and engaging in petty retaliation. The Bible commends the former and condemns the latter.[21] The principle of love surely includes within its sphere the protection of human life in the face of extreme violence.

So, what is going on here? Well, for whatever reason, the religious leaders of Jesus' day had twisted the Scripture to suit their own wants. But we do the same, do we not? We are often blinded by "self" in the name of religion, so that we see in the Scriptures the justification for homosexual clergy, on one extreme, or for church splits over carpet color, on the other. Here, they had taken this principle of divine justice, by which justice is to prevail in society, and applied it as their own pet principle to live by—as my right for retaliation. But in so doing, they had missed the very heart of God—that is to transform, and be seen through, the hearts of those who are His.

Here Jesus shocks us back to the original intent—not by telling us what it *is,* but by showing us what it is *not.* For by grasping for this supposed right, God's people had lost track of what is really right, as the second greatest commandment puts it: "Do not seek revenge...but love your neighbor as yourself" (Lv 19:18, NIV). It is this kind of love—selfless and long-suffering—that He shows us in what follows. So, Jesus here is not seeking to overturn the principle on which courts must rule, but to underscore the principle by which Christians must live. "But that's not what I *want!* I want pay-back, I want tit-for-tat, I want to get even." Yes, that is what I want, but it is not my right. It is just plain wrong.

ENDURING WRONG

SECOND: Next Jesus shows us what is *right,* and that is enduring the wrong of personal injustice. This is a wrong that, from God's perspective, is strangely right. This is illustrated in the four examples Jesus uses, that illustrate the heart we are to have. Each of these strikes at the heart of "rights" to show us the heart of Christ. Two of these, indeed, have become proverbial: "turning the other cheek" and "going the extra mile"—above and beyond the call of duty.

---

21 Compare Proverbs 24:11-12 with 24:29.

THE FIRST EXAMPLE is that of turning the other cheek: "But if anyone slaps you on the right cheek, turn to him the other also" (5:39). "But wait," you might say, "I have the *right* to repay. He hit me, I get to hit him back. It is only fair." Just watch children go from "play" to "fight." Yes, that is my natural instinct, and that is my natural desire. If, for example, I could step through these pages right now and give you a good, hard slap across the face, what would your instinct be? You might fight it, and successfully, but your face would flush and your eyes kindle, or you just might wallop me back. It is fighting nature. "But if I live like this, won't I be taken advantage of?" Probably. "And won't I be mocked as a weakling?" Probably. But which takes more strength? Again, if I were to step forward and sock you in the gut: which would take more strength, to sock me right back, or to stand there with hands down? I think you know the answer.

This is but one example of resisting the urge to retaliate. But we could expand this to anything that someone does that wrongs me, where I want to return the favor. It could be when someone cuts you off on the freeway. What is your first thought? It could be when someone defames or humiliates you. What do you want to do? Rise up and strike back! But Jesus calls us to something bigger, and something better; Jesus calls us to follow Him. And no, it is not natural... it is supernatural. As the apostle Peter writes:

> For this is a gracious thing, when, mindful of God, one endures sorrows while suffering unjustly. For what credit is it if, when you sin and are beaten for it, you endure? But if when you do good and suffer for it you endure, this is a gracious thing in the sight of God. For to this you have been called, because Christ also suffered for you, leaving you an example, so that you might follow in His steps. He committed no sin, neither was deceit found in His mouth. When He was reviled, He did not revile in return; when He suffered, He did not threaten, but continued entrusting Himself to Him who judges justly (1 Pt 2:19-23).

THE SECOND EXAMPLE might seem a little strange to us at first (5:40), about suing for our tunic: strange, because our clothing styles have radically changed; we do not wear tunics and cloaks anymore, but we do wear shirts and coats. But then, I think we get the picture. Here, someone is suing me for those very things that are closest to me, and that I really need. What would be my natural reaction to someone doing this to me? Outrage! But Jesus wants to develop in each of us *a heart that is willing to be wronged.* As the apostle Paul will say, "Why not rather be wronged?" (1 Cor 6:7). But, you might say, even according to the Scriptures, I have the legal *right* to keep my cloak. No one has the right to take that from me (see Ex 22:26). But then again, where is your heart; where is your attitude? Is it set on your self, your rights; or is it set on following Christ and trusting God? This is difficult. But this is what we are called to do, and it is a far better life being free from grasping.

THE THIRD EXAMPLE is captured in that all-familiar phrase: "going the extra mile"—though the original setting is far from ours (5:41). In Jesus' day, the Israelites were under Roman domination. One of the irritations of Roman rule was their right to compel ordinary citizens to carry their military baggage for one mile. You had no choice; it was forced upon you. How would you react in this case? Many would probably grumble, complain, and quietly curse until their duty was done—and not one step further! But then, Jesus tells us to willingly go double. "But I have the *right* to go no further. It is an injustice as it is!" But Jesus wants to develop in each of us not only a heart that is willing to be wronged, but also a desire to *go above and beyond the call of duty.*

So, let me ask: What is your (good) duty in your marriage? Husband, love your wife; wife, respect[22] your husband (Eph 5:33)—now, go above and beyond! Or, what is your (good) duty as children? "Honor your father and mother" (Eph 6:2)—now, go above and beyond! And what is your (good) duty as employers and employees (if I can borrow from the master-slave relationship)? Treat them fairly, work whole-heartedly (Col 3:23; 4:1)—now, go above and beyond! This is all too common, but do you do *only* what is required, and with a sour attitude—and not one bit further? Or on the other hand, what will people think when they see us not only willingly perform an often uncomfortable duty, but then go way beyond what is required? What will your spouse think? What will your employer think? Well, they will see a *difference.* They will see the

---

22 The term here is one that denotes reverence; literally, "fear" (φοβέω).

difference that the love of God makes in our hearts and lives—they will see the life of Christ.

THE LAST EXAMPLE is shocking as well: "Give to the one who begs from you" (5:42). Again, our natural reaction might be: "But I have the *right* to keep my own stuff. I earned it." True to a point; but there are two big attitude questions our Lord is seeking to address.

First, what is your attitude toward your possessions? Do you see all your stuff as "yours"? Or do you view it as God's stuff that has been entrusted to you? As the Scriptures tell us: "It is God who gives us the ability to produce wealth" (Dt 8:18); that "everything in the heavens and earth is His" (1 Chr 29:11); and that "without Him we can do nothing" (Jn 15:5).

Second, what is your attitude toward the needy? Do you see them as somebody else's problem, or their neediness as their own fault (and sometimes it is)? Or do you see them as humans made in the image of God, whom God Himself has placed in your pathway to help. Look again at the parable of the Good Samaritan. Now, there is one caveat here (and it is probably in all of your minds). There are some who are professional beggars, who refuse to work, etc. There are many of them around us. It takes great wisdom, but we are called to exercise it, and we should err on the side of giving. We should do so according to true need. For example, if a drunk asks you for money for food or bus fare, do not give him money—he will just use it for booze. Rather, buy him some food or put him on the bus. But this takes time and effort, and it is much easier just to ignore.

So, what are our "rights" to give up? What are our "wrongs" to endure? What Jesus wants to see is a heart that is willing to be wronged, that will go above and beyond. He wants to see a heart that is bigger than ourselves, that is generous to those in need, and that holds loosely to the stuff of this earth. Yes, it is a distinct and radical attitude shift away from self and toward Christ, away from "my rights" and toward "what is Jesus' way?" Remember, He laid down His life for us.

LOVE YOUR ENEMY
AS YOURSELF

(Matthew 5:43-48)

You have heard that it was said,
"You shall love your neighbor and hate your enemy."
But I say to you, Love your enemies and pray for those who persecute
you, so that you may be sons of your Father who is in heaven.
For He makes His sun rise on the evil and on the good,
and sends rain on the just and on the unjust.
For if you love those who love you, what reward do you have?
Do not even the tax collectors do the same?
And if you greet only your brothers, what more are you doing
than others? Do not even the Gentiles do the same?
You therefore must be perfect, as your heavenly Father is perfect.

W E have recently passed only the eighth anniversary of the 9-11 attacks that brought the Towers down and exposed our soft underbelly like no event since Pearl Harbor, so it should still be fresh on our minds. With the resurgence of the Taliban in Afghanistan, spilling over into Pakistan, with Bin Laden still on the loose, with the relentless and bloody suicide attacks in Iraq, the tyrant in North Korea, and the rise of that charismatic madman in Iran bent on nuclear ambition and threatening the destruction of Israel, we live in a world of real and serious enmity; we live in a time of clear and present danger.

We suffer as Americans; as Christians we suffer more. Here are a couple of fairly recent examples:

On April 18, 2007, we heard a report out of Turkey about three Christians who were brutally murdered. This was completely unpro-voked and only happened because of their faith. One was a German missionary, and the other two were Turkish converts from Islam, one of whom, by then, was an evangelical pastor. The details—even those that can be confirmed—are horrifying. They were tortured, stabbed, and their throats deeply slit. They left behind wives without husbands, children without fathers, churches without leaders; all were left behind to mourn...and pray.[23]

Here is another example that sticks out in one's mind, in which the Christian instinct of compassion was used as bait. According to Compass Direct, on September 3, 2006, some Hindu extremists in India's Karnataka state laid a trap for a Christian evangelist named Thomas. On his way to a church meeting that Sunday evening, Thomas and his wife saw the apparent victim of a motorcycle accident lying in the middle of the road. Thomas left his car to assist him, a good Christian and "Good Samaritan" thing to do. But as soon as he bent over the victim, the man threw chili powder into his eyes. Then a group of about fifteen Hindus hiding in the bushes jumped out and started physically and verbally attacking him. His wife said, "One of them came up to the car and told me that both of us would face a cruel death if we continued to preach in the village."

So what do you do? Give up and give in? *This Christianity just is not worth it.* Or rise up and strike back? *This Christian love just does not work.* Yet, the Scriptures tell us to love our neighbor. That is usually not a problem for us to comprehend or put into practice. But what if that neighbor hates us? That is a more difficult question to wrestle with. How, Lord, how? Jesus addresses the very issue of frequently living as Christians among people that hate us. I want to unwrap His words by way of two questions and answers that may surprise us a bit, for again they turn things upside-down from the way we are used to thinking and acting.

MY ENEMY IS MY NEIGHBOR

To the first question, "Who is my neighbor?" Jesus answers, in essence, that *my neighbor includes my enemy.* [24]

---

23 Reports of this incident (any many incidents daily) are widely publicized in Christian, secular, and international forums. For example, visit www.compassdirect.org.

24 An enemy bent on destroying the neighborhood is not, properly speaking, a neighbor. Notwithstanding, if it is within our power, God requires that we give water, food, or medical treatment even to such a vicious enemy.

Looking at the beginning of these verses again (5:43), we see that Jesus starts out with another one of His restatements of God's law where He says, "You have heard that it was said…but I say to you." But His quotation here is unique, for it is not clearly (or at least entirely) *from* God's law. The first half comes directly from the Old Testament (as expected). It is the second greatest commandment (Lv 19:18):

> You shall not take vengeance or bear a grudge against the sons of your own people, but you shall love your neighbor as yourself: I am the Lord.

But that is where the verse ends. There is no mention of hating your enemy. In fact, the second half of the quotation is nowhere to be found, as such, in any of the writings of the Old Testament. So, what is going on here?

Is it, perhaps, a fair representation of Old Testament teaching? Fair question. And certainly, when we come to Jesus, we come to something fuller—and as such, something better. There is a definite intensification and application of these commands in the life of God's people in this age of "grace *upon* grace," as John 1:16 describes it. But the highest ethical charge in the New Testament remains the same as that of the Old. The two great commands of the Old (love God, love each other) are the same great commands of the New. The essence has not changed. And, perhaps surprisingly, the Old Testament *does* talk about showing love to our enemies (we will see a little more of this later). So, "hate your enemy" is not what the Bible teaches.

Then what is going on here? As we have seen, Jesus has been addressing the common understanding of the Scriptures and their demands on our lives—the righteousness that God requires and heaven demands—as interpreted through the religious leaders, notably the scribes and Pharisees, the most impeccably righteous people in His day—at least outwardly. But Jesus said, "Unless your righteousness *exceeds* [these], you will *never* enter the kingdom of heaven" (5:20)—which leaves us all hopeless…apart from God's grace. They had externalized God's commands, made them manageable. "Don't murder, no problem; no adultery, no problem." But then Jesus pierces the depths and reveals the essence of the commands, forcing us to look at the underlying sin down to the level of the heart. At that level, we all break them horridly. There we are left exposed and hopeless...apart from God's grace. Not only must our righteousness exceed that of the most perfect people on the planet, it must also match the perfection of God Himself ("You therefore must be perfect, as your heavenly Father is perfect," 5:48). No one in his right mind will admit to that kind of perfection. As the Scriptures clearly teach: "All have sinned and fall short of the glory of God" (Rom 3:23)—which leaves us all hopeless...apart from God's grace.

But an ancient text from Jesus' day has been discovered that does indeed explicitly teach this very thing; it is one of the Dead Sea Scrolls. These are a group of religious writings—including much of the Scriptures—that were discovered sixty years ago at Qumran in the desert caves above the Dead Sea. The people there were a group of religious separatists (probably Essenes), who were extremely concerned about maintaining righteousness and holiness (the Pharisees were too liberal for them!). Their defining document, the Rule of the Community, began by instructing its followers to "seek God with a whole heart and soul, and do what is good and right." This sounds good so far, but then it goes on to command them to "love all the sons of light...and *hate* all the sons of darkness" (1 QS 1:1-11).[25] In our context, that might be worded: "Love all Christians...and hate all non-Christians."

Another representation of this mind-set is found in the Book of Sirach, part of the Apocrypha (made up of good religious books written between the times of the Testaments, but that are not part of the Bible):

> Give to the godly man, but do not help the sinner.
>   Do good to the humble, but do not give to the ungodly;
> hold back his bread, and do not give it to him,
>   lest by means of it he subdue you;
> for you will receive twice as much evil
>   for all the good which you do to him.
> For the Most high also hates sinners
>   and will inflict punishment on the ungodly.
> Give to the good man, but do not help the sinner (Sir 12:4-7).[26]

---

25 G. Vermes, *The Dead Sea Scrolls in English*, 3rd ed. (London: Penguin Books, 1987), 62 (emphasis added).

26 Bruce M. Metzger, ed., *The Oxford Annotated Apocrypha, Revised Standard Version*, expanded ed. (Oxford: Oxford University Press, Inc., 1977), 143.

But this is not what the Scriptures say, is it? No, they tell us (both Old and New): "If your enemy is hungry, feed him" (Prv 25:21; Rom 12:20).

Apparently however, many in Jesus' day had come to believe that if the Scriptures command us to *love* our neighbor, then it must likewise mean we are to *hate* our enemy. Sounds natural, does it not? It is an all-too-common deduction, but it is wrong, and it breeds wrong things. Here are two of the chief examples.

One: This mind-set of "love your neighbor, hate your enemy" breeds *separatism.* This was not just the people of Qumran. The Jews of Jesus' day had erected invisible walls of separation to keep away from the Samaritans they hated because they considered them unclean, as half-breeds and religious compromisers. So, they would even go the long way around (crossing over the Jordan) to avoid Samaritan territory in order to avoid contamination. We as Christians so easily fall into this as well—when we get too inward focused or too afraid of contamination by the world. Do we really care about the world or engage the world? Where, then, is the opportunity for Gospel entry and Gospel impact? If we take such an extreme stance of separatism, then the Great Commission is lost… or is no longer heard. "Go" is not just to the foreign field, it begins here at home.

Two: It breeds *violence.* The Zealots of Jesus' day were particularly fond of this.[27] Hatred of Rome's injustice served as the justification for their violent ways, notably, their bloody assassinations of Roman soldiers and Roman collaborators. We certainly see this, and in particular today in the violence being perpetrated in the name of Islam. Even Pope Benedict's remarks in September 2006, quoting a medieval emperor's assessment of Islam as inherently violent (that it had brought "only things evil and inhuman")…was met with more violence! This sad irony was strangely lost on the public and on the world of Islam. For example, in the aftermath of these words, a Catholic nun was murdered in Somalia; a priest was beheaded in Iraq; and in Gaza and the West Bank, Christian churches were burned. Then Pakistan's foreign ministry spokeswoman, Tasnim Aslam, said that *anyone who describes Islam "as intolerant encourages*

---

27 See, for example, Josephus' descriptions of their activities in *The Jewish War*, book 4, chapters 3-6.

violence"! Sometimes we get blinded, too. An extreme example is when the injustice of abortion has been used as a justification for the bombing of abortion clinics. But it is wrong to let our rightful hatred against sin cause us to become hurtful in our attitudes or words against sinners.

This is the natural response to this ethic. If you live by the ethic of "love neighbor and hate enemy," you will naturally tend toward separatism and violence. To state the obvious, neither of these are virtues. We see this in our current world situation in a big way, but it is not far from each of us. None of us is immune from falling into this trap. Therefore, Christians must not hate their enemies, neither by harboring hatred, which is murder in the heart, nor through acts of revenge. The Holy Spirit enables us not to sin in these ways.

Jesus says, "Love your enemies" (5:44). With these words, Jesus shocks us by asserting the unthinkable: *that we are to love those who hate us.* In the very context of these words (5:46-47), Jesus defines these enemies for us. He does so in such a way as to include both those whom we would naturally consider our enemies—the Gentiles (in the political-national sense) as well as those whom we would naturally consider our neighbors (those who belong to our people-group, but who may have an interior disposition of hatred toward us, or we may have toward them). Especially notable here are the "tax collectors," who were among their own people (technically and narrowly neighbors), but who were despised, and considered greedy and oppressive traitors, thus, their enemies.

This concept of neighbor is not foreign to the Old Testament context of the command itself. Jesus takes it further and makes it clearer, but the kernel is still unmistakably there. Notice the following verses from Leviticus 19—and their intentional pairing and framing of the issue:

> You shall not hate your brother in your heart, but you shall reason frankly with your neighbor, lest you incur sin because of him. You shall not take vengeance or bear a grudge against the sons of your own people, but *you shall love your neighbor as yourself:* I am the LORD (Lv 19:17-18).

> When a stranger sojourns with you in your land, you shall not do him wrong. You shall treat the stranger who sojourns with you as the native among you, and *you shall love him as*

yourself, for you were strangers in the land of Egypt; I am the LORD your God (Lv 19:33-34).

Even in the context of Leviticus 19, "neighbor" is broader than its immediate parallels "brother" and "the sons of your own people." It includes everyone within the community—even "strangers" (גֵּרִים). Against such immigrants we may feel a sense of suspicion and enmity, and our natural tendency, as our Lord makes clear, may be to *do him wrong* (Lv 19:33). But both fellow Israelite and foreign immigrant are to be loved in like manner, "as yourself."

In our own context, loving the *immigrant* may take different forms. The legal immigrant is clearly a Biblical stranger and deserves equal treatment with all other neighbors. However, in the case of the illegal immigrant, it is certainly not unloving to enforce the laws of the land and to inhibit criminal behavior—indeed, it is incumbent upon our government and citizenry to do so. Regardless of this, however, every human being is to be treated as one's "neighbor," with the respect and care that is due to those who are made in the image of God (see Jas 3:9-10; 1 Pt 2:17). So, for example, if an illegal and his dependents are in need of water, food, shelter, clothing, comfort, or medical care, the Christian is duty bound to meet that physical need (Rom 12:20). At the same time, he is duty bound to cooperate with the local authorities and national laws. This is one aspect of loving your neighbor—and loving your enemy—as yourself.

Yet, it is not loving to allow someone to perpetrate evil if it is in our power to stop it. Stopping evil is loving to one's other neighbors. It is even loving the enemy, since stopping the enemy limits the grounds of judgment he will incur and may give him the opportunity to repent. Stopping evil is, therefore, an aspect of loving your neighbor as yourself. Christians are truly not to hate our neighbors, even our enemies. Neither are we to rejoice over their fall (Prv 24:17). Although we must defend against vicious attack, even those who would destroy us must not receive our hatred in return (Rom 12:17). Rather, if our enemy needs food or water, we give it; if he is in need of medical attention, we provide it, if it lies within our power to do so. This, at a very basic level, is what it means to love your enemy as yourself. And so, too, we are transformed from harboring resentment to instead putting love into action.

Thus, when Jesus taught us to love our enemies, it was not fundamen-tally anything new. It was, nonetheless, unthinkable. How can we do that? We will look at what that means in a moment. First let me note what this is not. It is not the issue of public justice or of self-defense—whether that be defending against neighborhood thugs, fighting terrorists, or sentencing criminals.[28] Rather, it is interpersonal. It is our governing principle, the Christian ethic of how we are to live with one another in our day-to-day lives. As the Scriptures declare, there is a difference between personal ethics and civil ethics.

This is illustrated in the instructive juxtaposition between the latter part of Romans 12 and the first part of Romans 13. In Romans 12:19, Christians are forbidden from taking vengeance, but are rather to defer to God's wrath and do good: "Leave it to the wrath of God...Vengeance is mine, I will repay." Instead, we are counseled: "If your enemy is hungry, feed him; if he is thirsty, give him something to drink" (Rom 12:20). This is to be our personal ethic, and is in concord with the second greatest commandment: "You shall not take vengeance...but you shall love your neighbor as yourself" (Lv 19:18). In this way, we "overcome evil with good" (Rom 12:21).

But governmental ethics is the ethics of vengeance, as God's servants, against this very evil. Concerning the state and the office of the civil mag-istrate, the apostle Paul writes: "For he is the servant of God, an avenger who carries out God's wrath (ἔκδικος εἰς ὀργὴν) on the wrongdoer" (Rom 13:4). The state is entrusted with taking vengeance, and we are to defer to that wrath and do good. These are complementary callings: Just as we are not to take vengeance and instead to do good—knowing that God will take vengeance on the day of wrath on all who remain unre-pentant of their evil (Rom 12:19-20)—so the state is to take vengeance and to commend the good that we do (Rom 13:3-4). Thus, whereas the Christian is to be governed fundamentally by the principle of love, the

---

28 It is not Biblical simply to lump together irritation with intent to do egregious harm. If Christians are not allowed to wield the sword against God's enemies (though we love them), then we cannot represent God before men in the civil arena. Personal defense and the defensive war are Biblically non-antithetical with Christian love. This is one of the many truths in tension that Christians are called to embrace: for example, the Bible vaunts the man of valor and the meek; justice and mercy; law and grace; faith and works; one God in three Persons.

state is to be governed fundamentally by the principle of recompense, that is, punishing evil and promoting good.[29] But here in this passage, Jesus is not addressing questions of public justice; He is addressing the principle that is to govern our interpersonal relationships. To this issue Jesus says, "Love your enemy."

Again, we are not dealing here with *state* issues—like how we are to respond to the Muslim terrorists. Nor are we dealing with a degree of evil that is blatantly vicious and violent. Murderers, rapists, and robbers (among others) are to be actively opposed, apprehended, and given their proper judicial sentence.[30] But this is not the kind of enmity that Jesus is addressing here; other Scriptures speak to that.[31] Rather, Jesus is confronting us with our more *ordinary* enemies, those people we naturally hate (in that context, the "Gentiles," the "tax collectors," Matthew 5:46-47).

So then, who is my enemy? This might seem like an easy question, a no-brainer. We have all got some preconceived *enemies* in our own minds, do we not? It is the current political administration! It is our *neighbor*—whose dog howls all night, who plays his rock music too loudly, who never returns the tools he borrows, etc. Or, as I mentioned in the last section, it could be the person who cuts us off on the freeway, or defames or humiliates us in public, about which our instinct is to return the favor, tit-for-tat. But when the Scriptures say, "Love your *neighbor* as yourself," what it also means is, "Love your *enemy* as yourself." If we are to feed and medically treat a mortal enemy, surely we must show kindness to those who merely annoy us.

We do not like that. But this is precisely what Jesus was getting at, in a backward way, in the Parable of the Good Samaritan. The Samaritan

---

29 Adapted from John N. Day, *Crying for Justice: What the Psalms Teach Us about Mercy and Vengeance in an Age of Terrorism* (Grand Rapids: Kregel Publications, 2005), 126, n. 24. Also, consult this work for a Christian defense of imprecatory prayers in their appropriate place.

30 It is important, once more, to distinguish between enemies as those who harbor hatred against another, and those who act upon that hatred. Such action is understood as warfare, whether by a people or a single person. There is no antagonism between loving one's adversary and defending oneself, including the use of lethal force, to stop an imminent attack—either as a single person or a group of people. Opposing another with lethal force to stop a lethal attack stops another from greater sin and therefore greater judgment. Such defense is in itself loving one's neighbor as oneself.

31 See, for example, Genesis 9:5-6; Deuteronomy 22:25-27; Luke 23:40-41.

was the *enemy*,[32] and yet Jesus showed what it means to be a neighbor to the one who would naturally hate him. Jesus is saying that this is what it must mean to keep the commandment.

> "Which of these three, do you think, proved to be a neighbor to the man who fell among the robbers?"
>
> He said, "The one who showed him mercy."
>
> And Jesus said to him, "You go, and do likewise" (Lk 10:36-37).

In this parable, Jesus drives home that the heart of the command, "love your neighbor," includes implicitly within it "love your enemy." The one who is in need, and whose need I may meet, is my neighbor—whoever that may be. He may still be my enemy, but now my enemy becomes my neighbor.

And this is where we see the difference. As Jesus explains (in 5:46): we all naturally love those who love us. But love that is from God must go beyond that. This is where we see, in our own day, the striking difference between Islam and Christianity—between one religion that calls its followers to "hate their enemies"[33] and the other which calls us to "love our enemies." This, too, is one of the challenges we face today—to love those under the darkness of Islam that they might come to see the light of Christ.

LOVE IS SOMETHING YOU DO

Now we come to the second question: *What does it mean to love my enemy?* And to this question, Jesus answers: *Love is something you do.*

In general we tend to think of love as something we *feel*—that mushy feeling we get toward another. We fall *in* love, we fall *out* of love. As

---

32 There was a long history of antipathy and antagonism between the Jews and the Samaritans. The Samaritans were considered "unclean" because they were racial half-breeds and religious compromisers; they did not keep the Law in the manner the Jews demanded; and they maintained a status of opposition to the truth, stemming from the rebuilding of the walls of Jerusalem and the temple under Ezra and Nehemiah.

33 Qur'an sura 60, verse 4 says: "There is a goodly pattern for you in Abraham and those with him, when they told their folk: Lo! we are guiltless of you and all that ye worship beside Allah. We have done with you. And there hath arisen between us and you hostility and hate forever until ye believe in Allah only." So here, Abraham, whom Islamic theology considers a Muslim, is given approval when he tells his idol-worshipping family that he hates them unless and until they become Muslims.

Christians, we tend to think of love as something we *say* (and we get really good at saying it). I am not saying that is wrong. Love is something we should say, and love is something we should feel. But love is more than that—love is something we *do*. It is interesting that Leviticus 19, which brings us the second greatest commandment: "love your neighbor as yourself" (Lv 19:18), spends most of the chapter describing what this love looks like in real life situations. For example, pay your workers in a timely manner, show respect for the elderly, etc. And the New Testament also speaks in this same way: "This is the love of God, that we keep His commandments" (1 Jn 5:3). Love is not proven in our words or in our feelings, but in our actions. Husbands and wives, especially, can attest to that. Our Lord illustrates this truth in two examples that show us what it means to love our enemies.

First, in the command for *prayer.* As in all things, love begins in the heart. The heart is revealed in what we wish for, or what we pray for. Jesus says, "Love your enemies…and *pray* for those who persecute you" (5:44). This means that we pray for their welfare: not that they will succeed in their evil, but that the Lord will truly bless them, especially that they will come to know the love of God in Jesus. But do we actually pray like this? Is this our instinct when wronged? We see this most profoundly on the lips of Christ Himself while hanging on the cross—that height of human cruelty and undeserved enmity. And Jesus *prayed,* "Father, forgive them, for they know not what they do" (Lk 23:34)! If our Lord could pray that *then,* what keeps us from praying that way *now* in our own pain and injustice? If I love my enemies, I will surely want to pray for their salvation: that they might see Jesus, and not judgment! But do I?

Second, in the analogy of *kindness.* One of the clearest ways to show love is in deeds of kindness. This is how God shows it to us, and this is how we are to show it to one another. Even here, Jesus establishes the command for *loving* our enemies on the analogy of the *kindness* of God. Jesus says, "Love your enemies…for He makes His sun rise on the evil and on the good, and sends rain on the just and on the unjust" (5:44-45). We see this throughout the Scriptures. Here are a couple of examples:

Deuteronomy 10:18-19 tells us that we are to "Love the sojourner" (or *immigrant* or "stranger," גֵר) because God Himself "loves the sojourner, giving him food and clothing." Our love, like our Lord's words to us in

Matthew 5:44-45, is based upon God's pattern of provision. He does not simply command us; He commands us out of His own example. In those days, even more so than in our own, the temptation was toward mistreatment and feelings of suspicion. But we are still called to kindness.

Exodus 23:4-5 tells us in very practical terms:

> If you meet your enemy's ox or his donkey going astray [this would be like his truck or tractor in our own day: it was his transportation and livelihood], you shall bring it back to him. If you see the donkey *of one who hates you* lying down under its burden, you shall refrain from leaving him with it [which is what we would naturally do: drive on by, *he got what he deserves*]; you shall rescue it with him.

That is, if you see the car of someone who hates your guts (calls you names, treats you like dirt) stalled on the side of road, you must stop and assist. This is love, and this is what Jesus calls us to.

This is *the difference.* We have seen this difference demonstrated on a massive scale in the aftermath of those two huge disasters on the far side of the world: the monstrous tsunami centered off Indonesia in December 2004 (with a death toll over 200,000), and the devastating earthquake in northern Pakistan in October 2005 (with a death toll over 80,000). What is striking is that these countries are two of the worst, when it comes to the active persecution of Christians by Muslims, and yet, it was relief from Christians around the world that flooded in. This is "love your enemy as yourself."

One of the missionary families that my church supports ministers in Thailand, and was there to assist in the aftermath of the tsunami that racked the resort area of Phuket. They reported that the largely Buddhist population stayed away for fear of the ghosts, and the Muslims stayed away as well. But the Christians were not afraid; Christians care, and so Christians came. In the wake of God's stunning devastation came the flood of God's grace through God's people. Now (the wonders of God), there are over sixty churches formed in that area, where there were almost none before. As the Scriptures tell us, the Lord brings good out of evil; and so do His people, if we *image* Him.

Jesus' command to "love your enemies" is indeed a radical command —perhaps the most radical of them all. But here Jesus does not overturn the Old Testament (as with the others He has addressed). Rather He intensifies it, for *He came not to abolish, but to fulfill* (Mt 5:17). God teaches us by His example as well as by His Words; and Jesus reveals both the heart of God and the heart of God's commands, so that "love your neighbor as yourself" also means "love your enemy as yourself." This love essentially means that I will show kindness whenever I can because the one who is in need, and whose need I can meet, *is* my *neighbor*—even if he is my *enemy.*

12

THE DANGER OF
PUBLIC RELIGION

(Matthew 6:1-6)

*Beware of practicing your righteousness before other people
in order to be seen by them,
for then you will have no reward from your Father who is in heaven.
Thus, when you give to the needy, sound no trumpet before you,
as the hypocrites do in the synagogues and in the streets,
that they may be praised by others.
Truly, I say to you, they have received their reward.
But when you give to the needy,
do not let your left hand know what your right hand is doing,
so that your giving may be in secret.
And your Father who sees in secret will reward you.
And when you pray, you must not be like the hypocrites.
For they love to stand and pray in the synagogues
and at the street corners, that they may be seen by others.
Truly, I say to you, they have received their reward.
But when you pray, go into your room and shut the door
and pray to your Father who is in secret.
And your Father who sees in secret will reward you.*

How often have you heard the sentiment: "Religion is a private matter.
If that is what you need, fine; but keep it out of the public sphere"?
Too often we hear politicians themselves claim: "Sure, I'm a Christian and
I personally believe that [for example] abortion is wrong, but I should not
let my religious views influence my approach to public policy." Indeed, in
our increasingly secularized society, it has become the common dogma

that religious faith is all right or at least tolerated, as long as you keep it to yourself or in church, but that it somehow becomes "dangerous" when it is allowed to affect your public life. Too often we have been cowed into submission, although now we have begun to push back. As we rightly understand, religion that is real can never be divorced from our public life because Christ is Lord of *all* my life.

Yet, there is an aspect of this charge that is true. Religion *can* be a dangerous thing. Notice how Jesus begins here with "Beware" (6:1). That is, there is a danger here. In particular, there is a danger to public religion. But it is not what people often think. The danger is not, as the secularists perceive, that of bringing religious convictions into the public arena, or even whether we should be able to question Darwinism in our schools or post the Ten Commandments in our courts. Nor is the issue here the fanaticism exemplified by the Muslim extremists, though that is indeed dangerous—even deadly. What Jesus means is something completely different, and quite surprising. What is the danger?

In these next verses of His sermon (6:1-18), Jesus confronts our stubborn human tendency toward "image" religion—religion that is characterized by outward show and hypocrisy. He does so by looking at the three chief examples of piety in His day: alms, prayer, and fasting. In discussing charitable giving and public prayer, He begins by establishing the *principle* of piety—that it is the motive that matters, and then the *practice* of piety—what it looks like when no one is looking. What Jesus emphasizes for us again is that real religion must be seated *in* the heart and lived out *from* the heart.

THE PRINCIPLE OF PIETY

Right at the start, Jesus lays down the principle of piety: it is the motive that matters. "Beware of practicing your righteousness before other people in order to be seen by them . . . " (6:1). Before we look at that principle, I want us first to notice the presumption about such religious expression. The *given* is this: that it is a good thing, and that we will do it. Why say this? It is because Jesus Himself calls it "righteousness." You could call it "doing what is right"—and that is always a good thing. Also, in all three examples Jesus repeatedly says *when* and not *IF*. He says: "*When* you give" (6:2,3), "*when* you pray" (6:5,6,7), "*when* you fast" (6:16, 17). It is not *optional*, but something He assumes we will do. There are many people who say they are Christians, but we do not see them seeking after God or see changes in their lives. We can *say* we are Christians, but if people cannot *see* us live as Christians, there is an underlying problem, because for Jesus, this is the *given*.

So we are to do it, yes, but there is more. This is where the principle we often miss comes in: that we are to do the right things for the right reasons—for the praise of God and not the praise of man. This is the question of motive. As Jesus brings out, it is the *motive* behind our piety that makes all the difference—makes it real or makes it fake. But this is something only God can judge…and He does. The Father *sees* (Mt 6:4, 6, 18). Notice that this is the issue of the heart again. *Am I doing this to please God or to look good?*

Their motive was to "be praised by others" (6:2), to "be seen by others" (6:5). This is a fundamentally selfish motive, which always seems to be our problem. We see it in the extreme in the Islamic suicide bombers who receive great acclaim by their religious communities including their own families. They believe that they may have the prospect of instant heaven with beautiful virgins. That might sound as if they are doing it for God's reward, but it really is nothing more than doing it for man's acclaim and their own selfish desires. Jesus had earlier stated that we should let our light (the light of Christ shining through us, *real* religion) so shine before others "that they may see your good works and give glory to your Father who is in heaven" (5:16). Does the broader world glorify God when innocent people are blown to bits? No. As I said, that is the extreme. But it is the same selfish root in each of our hearts. It is seductive, for who gets the glory in the good things we do? Whose praise do we seek?

So then, let me ask: What is my motive? This is a *heart* question, and I need to ask it in everything I do.

To take one example: as a pastor I have to consciously pray this to God every week as I prepare to preach. It is a weighty matter, and the temptation is to try to craft a message that will impress my congregation. That is a trap, and it is wrong. Yes, I am supposed to do my best; but it must be my best *for God.* Yes, I should seek to communicate in a compelling manner, but so that hearts are gripped by *God* and directed toward *God.*

Then there is something that is common to us all, doing nice things for others. That is a good thing we are all supposed to do and do all the time: "Be kind to one another" (Eph 4:32). But when we do these nice things, are we expecting some form of recognition or return? Or do we do them simply as part of our lives lived in the presence of God and for His gaze and reward alone? Husbands and wives provide an example. When you do something nice for your wife, do you do it so that she will do something nice for *you?* Or do you do it simply because loving your wife is the right thing to do before God, "as Christ loved the church and gave Himself up for her" (Eph 5:25). Wife, do you treat your husband with respect so that he will give you the kind of attention you want, or simply and sincerely because Christ calls you to do so? It is the question of motive, and for Jesus, it is the motive that matters.

THE PRACTICE OF PIETY

From the principle, Jesus describes the practice of true piety and shows what it looks like when no one is looking.

The first example Jesus uses (in 6:2-4) is that of giving to the needy—something that everyone recognizes as really good, if not the best of religion. These were ostensibly good religious people...and they let everyone know just how good and religious they were. They were (literally and figuratively) "tooting their own horn." But we might not see a problem here. "Hey, the needy are helped and the givers are congratulated. What is the problem?" The problem then, and why Jesus calls them "hypocrites," is that their focus was not on God, but on themselves. They were supposedly doing something righteous before God, and yet they were doing it for the praise of other people. Do you see the disconnect? It is a self-focus. This kind of public religion is dangerous—because it exposes a heart of hypocrisy, and hypocrisy is always a dangerous thing.

Speaking of which, this is the first of Jesus' many denouncements against religious hypocrisy, and this is something we need to hear. Furthermore, it is not just a religion issue, but a *human* issue; it is something we *all* need to hear. You have probably heard the old banter: "I don't want anything to do with church; the church is full of hypocrites." "Well, come on in; there is always room for one more!"

What is hypocrisy? In its most basic sense, it is pretending to be something you are not (the word in Greek is actually the term for "actor").

Here it is deep, for it probably involves even self-deception.[34] "Look at all the good things we do, look at how *good* the public *knows* we are!" We can be lulled into thinking that we are right before God, but if our hearts are not seeking God and relying on His grace, and instead are seeking self and relying on our goodness, then we are in the greatest danger—the danger of damnation.

We fall into the same trap. In our society, we have lots of philanthropists, who give large sums of money for great causes to benefit humanity. Everyone knows it because they give with their name attached and we praise them for it. And they have their reward, but it does not give them any better standing before God than the needy they helped. For salvation is by grace not works. Too often, however, we do the same thing in our churches. How much fund raising is done, or large donation items solicited, with "names attached"? What is your incentive for giving? If we only give because we get some recognition for it, then *we* are as hypocritical as they were.

Instead, the kind of piety Jesus looks for is one that He calls "secret": to freely give and render aid without anyone else needing to know. The way Jesus describes it, you almost keep it secret from yourself ("do not let your left hand know what your right hand is doing," 6:3). It should be both low profile and second nature. This combination of quiet generosity reveals the character of a grateful heart. If we recognize that all we *are* is by His grace. That we were helpless in our need, and yet He gave His Son to save us. And that all we *have* is by His grace, that it is from Him and for Him. Then we will freely give as a matter of course, and it will not matter if anyone knows.

The second example (in 6:5-6) is similar: they were *praying to impress,* and to impress with their spirituality. But God is not impressed. He looks for true and humble faith, no matter how that is expressed.

We are not immune from this temptation to hypocrisy in our prayer life either. How often do we pray in public to impress other people, to make it sound good, to make us look good? It is expected to be pretty, or holy, or profound. But who is supposed to be listening? Who is the audience? If it is prayer, then it is supposed to be prayer...to God. And

---

34 Compare with the description of sin's spiral in 2 Timothy 3:13.

God wants to see a *heart* of thankfulness or trust, not just hear inspiring words, though such words are great—if they come from the *heart*.

A word to pastors especially. They are asked to pray at occasions of all sorts, as well as in church—because they are the *professionals*. It is part of what they do. They are supposed to do it better and more effectively. But anyone can pray, anyone can speak to their heavenly Father, anytime and anywhere. The prayer of any Christian is powerful and effective (Jas 5:16). Simple is often best, as we will see in the Lord's Prayer, and bumbling is okay. The Spirit speaks through our groanings (Rom 8:26).

On the other side, how many of us feel too embarrassed to pray in public because we feel we will mess up or be judged because our prayer was not pretty, or holy, or profound? Those who judge on such terms must repent of their hypocrisy. Those who are afraid of that judgment must confess their timidity. Both of these are living for the praise of man, not the praise of God—and it is this motive that matters.

The kind of piety Jesus looks for is one that He again calls "secret," for the measure of true piety is what it looks like when no one is looking (except God, of course). This is not to condemn public prayer, but it must arise from a foundation of private prayer where no one is listening and no one is watching but God Himself. Remember how Jesus used to get away from the crowds to be alone with His Father? If even our Lord did that, then how much more do *we* need to develop a lifestyle of private prayer and communion with God? This has often been called "quiet time"—a time set apart to be alone with God (whether in a room or on a walk). Without this, our spiritual life begins to die, for it is His Spirit that is our life.

So, what is the danger of public religion? As Jesus underscores, the danger is missing God's reward: "for then you will have *no reward* from your Father who is in heaven" (6:1). Religious scandals are the worst, whether that is the televangelist scandals of twenty years ago, or the pedophilia scandals in the Catholic church more recently. Now we rightly cannot—and should not—keep our Christianity a secret. But if our religiosity is for show, if we are nothing but hypocrites, pretending to please God when we are really only pleasing ourselves, then we are in danger at two levels. First, there is the danger of damnation, for without the quickening of the Spirit there is no forgiveness of sins, so missing God's reward at that level is missing heaven. But also the danger of trading the praise of God for that of man is seductive to us all, when it is God's praise that really matters. Each day we live in the presence of God, though we often do not live like it, or even think that way. But one day we will all stand before the presence of God to answer for this life. Let us not live as though the universe revolves around *me*. Let us live for His applause: "Well done, good and faithful servant!...enter into the joy of your Master" (Mt 25:21, 23).

THE BASICS OF PRAYER

(Matthew 6:7-15)

And when you pray,
do not heap up empty phrases as the Gentiles do,
for they think that they will be heard for their many words.
Do not be like them, for your Father knows what you need
before you ask Him. Pray then like this:

Our Father in heaven,
hallowed be Your name.
Your kingdom come,
Your will be done,
on earth as it is in heaven.
Give us this day our daily bread,
and forgive us our debts,
as we also have forgiven our debtors.
And lead us not into temptation,
but deliver us from evil.

For if you forgive others their trespasses,
your heavenly Father will also forgive you,
but if you do not forgive others their trespasses,
neither will your Father forgive your trespasses.

As Christians, we are to be known as men and women and boys and girls of prayer. Our lives are to be lives of prayer, and the life of prayer is the life lived close to God. Yet, if prayer is such an integral part of our Christian lives, how do we grasp it? What are the basics of prayer? Jesus says, "Pray then like this" (6:9).

Jesus first sets this in contrast to a couple of ways we are *not* supposed to pray. Do *not* pray like this: first, openly (as we saw in the previous chapter), like the Jewish hypocrites (6:5), "that they may be seen by others"—using prayer as religious show; and second, like the Gentiles, heaping up "empty phrases"—using prayer as pious arm-twisting (6:7). This was seen in their lengthy incantations and prayer formulas by which the gods would be obligated to answer in a certain way. But we fall into this same trap as well, do we not, and are sometimes deceived by religious people? Anytime we succumb to the mind-set that we should pray a certain formula to achieve certain results, we have fallen into this trap—one that domesticates God and imprisons us from the life of prayer to which Jesus calls us. Examples of this are when Catholics are instructed to pray by the Rosary saying one "Our Father" and ten "Hail Marys," simply by rote; or when a charismatic leader tries to convince you to "pray with *this* miracle prayer cloth" which you can buy from him; or anytime that we are told to "say these words and do these things, and God will answer the way you want." But not only is God not impressed by showy words; God cannot be manipulated.

So, Jesus calls us in these verses to pray *simply* (6:7-8); He subscribes to the method we call KISS: "Keep It Simple, Stupid." What follows (6:9-13) is an expansion on this, a beautiful example in its simplicity, of what Jesus is talking about. As an aside, it is rightly called the Lord's Prayer, because it is the example set down by our Lord Himself. Some prefer to call it the Disciples' Prayer, since it is the model prayer *we* are to pray. We could also call it a Child's Prayer, for the way our Lord sets it up is in the very relationship of Father and child. And our Lord lays it out in the way that a child could grasp. A child is often our model for faith. So, what are the basics of prayer?

Built on Relationship

The first thing we see is the issue of relationship. This hits us *first* and it should hit us *hard*—in a truly amazing way. Jesus opens up by saying, "Our Father in heaven" (6:9). We may have gotten used to brushing over this without realizing its tremendous significance, but we must stop and ponder this, for it is truly a powerful statement. Jesus tells us that the basis of our prayer is this beautiful relationship of Father and child. It is a very special and tender relationship. It is also a relationship that sets the stage, the mood, and the parameters for all that follows. There are a couple of things here for us to notice particularly.

The Honor of "Father"

FIRST is that this indeed is a tremendous privilege and a beautiful relationship. We might not at first notice what a tremendous privilege and relationship this is!—either because we think wrongly of Him, or because we are so used to it. Those of you who are parents will understand this— how the sweetest words we can hear our children say, as we are coming through the door from work, is "Papa!" or "Daddy!" So this is what we are to see. Do you realize what an awesome thing this is?

How do you normally think of God? What is your picture of Him? Distant and uncaring (but He is not some "force"), or judgmental and harsh (but He is not mean), or doting and okay with whatever makes you happy (but He is not "grandfather")... or do you think of Him as "Father"? How do you normally begin your prayers? Almighty, eternal, holy (which are all true and good)... or "Father"?

Or perhaps you had a rotten father or have a rotten picture of what a father is? As Jesus presents it to us, this term is meant to portray entirely positive images. But it must be granted that there are many today for whom the word "father" brings to mind nothing but negative thoughts, because their earthly fathers abused them or abandoned them. But those men are not our heavenly Father, who is all to us—and more—of what a true father ought to be.

So, let us think rightly, and let us never take it for granted. We often say the Lord's Prayer in our liturgies, and often open our corporate prayers with words like: "Gracious heavenly Father." Do we realize what we are saying? I do not know of any other religion that has as its characteristic picture and designation for God, "Father." Other religions may say Creator, Great Spirit, Almighty, All-Compassionate, etc., but not "Father." This is telling and tremendous. He is the one "in heaven"—transcendent, God *beyond*...and yet He comes close to us by His grace.

Even in the Old Testament, God was referred to as "our Father" in the sense that He formed us (Is 64:8), but that was not the way they were called to address Him. This innovation of grace came from our Lord

Himself. He came as the Son, and always addressed God as His "Father," and directed us to know God as our "Father." As "the Son of God," He elevates us all into this relationship—into the liberty of "the sons of God" (Rom 8:14), so that we may cry: "Abba! Father!" (Rom 8:15).

Thus, there is a distinct privilege and intimacy in addressing *God* as Father. Not in any trivial way, certainly, but this is how our Lord invites us to come to God. And we do not come alone; notice He says, "Our." It is an intensely personal relationship; but we are not meant to live a private Christianity, contrary to what we may think. We are reminded that we are *meant* to live in Christian community, to worship and fellowship together, to consider ourselves "family" as exemplified in the earliest Christian practice of *koinonia*. For if God is our Father, then we are all brothers and sisters.

THE HONOR OF FATHERHOOD

SECOND: Knowing God as "Father" should call us both to honor fatherhood and to be honorable fathers.

This is not a very popular notion today. Just look at our sitcoms, both old and new: whether it is the harsh and domineering Archie Bunker or the slew of dolts and wimps that flood our TVs today, they are not funny, they are sickening. Just look at our society, in which men are considered largely unnecessary. That attitude makes its impact, especially on our boys—the men of the next generation. Just look at many of our inner cities, where abandonment and abuse is epidemic. These are increasing problems, and, as Christians, we must work to reverse these trends. God presents Himself as our Father, and so we should honor fatherhood. God presents what it means to be a father, and so we should seek to be honorable fathers.

Fathers, in particular, who confess God as "Father" are an encouragement for us to live as a reflection of the Father. Our children should grow up knowing the love of their heavenly Father by seeing the example of their earthly father. Among other things, He provides and cares for us (Mt 6:31-33). Do we as fathers do likewise? He shows us compassion (Ps 103:13). Is this what our children see? He disciplines us, but for our good (Heb 12:10). Is this what our children receive?

BRINGING OUR REQUESTS

So, the *basis* of our prayer is *relationship;* but the *body* of the prayer is *request*—and in two directions. The reason we are invited into the presence of God is because He is our Father and we are His children. But the bulk of the Lord's Prayer—the "nuts and bolts" of what Jesus teaches us about prayer—is that we come bringing our requests to Him. It is like the speech of children to their parents, who know what they need even before they ask (6:8). After the opening address, this prayer consists of six requests: the first three are directed toward God for His glory as indicated by the repeated "Your"; the last three are directed toward us for our good, as indicated by the repeated "us." To note this difference in fundamental direction, I have called them "praise" and "petition."

PRAISE

Granted, we too often tend to skip this aspect of prayer and go straight to the things we think we need or at least want. But Jesus puts "praise" first, and we need to take that to heart—that a direction toward *God* (rather than toward *me*) must always be first in our lives. What we see in these "praise requests" is that they are directed both *to* God, and to where our hearts need to be in relation to Him.

Our first reflex should be that of *reverence.* Jesus says, "hallowed be Your name" (6:9)—or in different language, "May Your name be treated as holy." This is an attitude of reverence at two levels.

First in our *speech:* Many Jews have taken this to an extreme by refusing to even pronounce the name of God. Many Americans, however, treat God's name as a trifle; even some Christians freely say: "O my God!" We ought to speak God's name, but only as it truly is—special.

But it certainly means more than this. This attitude of reverence should be reflected as well in our *actions.* We understand from the Scriptures that God's name is a reflection of who He is. Thus, we could say, "May *You* be shown proper reverence." This involves all my life, for all my life points to God—either to honor or to shame Him. Even as the Scriptures tell us the first commandment for children is to "Honor your father and your mother" (Ex 20:12), so it is with us and our heavenly Father. What do people see when they see me? Do they see hypocrisy or a double life—how does that hold Him up? Do they see blatant sins without repentance—which the Scriptures say "profane My holy name" (for example, in Lv 20:3)? Or do I seek to honor and reverence Him in all I say and do?

Our next response should be *submission.* Submission has been given a bad name in our day, whether through the radical feminist movement, or through the radical arm of Islam. The word "islam" itself means "submission," the key element of that religion—as opposed to Christianity, whose key is "love"! But when we understand that we are coming before the *King* of the universe, who works all things together for the *good* of those who love Him (Rom 8:28), then we can better see how this attitude of willing submission must be our natural response.

Jesus says, "Your kingdom come" (6:10). When we look all around us and see the advances of Satan's kingdom, the evils of murder, rape, and bloodshed, or the ravages of disease, death, and destroyed relationships, not to mention our own personal struggles with our frailty and sin, then the ache of our hearts, our sighs, and our cries ought to be (as the Scriptures themselves end): "Even so, come, Lord Jesus" (Rv 22:20, KJV)! This we await with longing, but it is also very close. "Your kingdom come" must begin in our hearts. Do others see that our lives are ruled by Him? Our prayer should be: Lord, let me show forth Your kingdom here and now.

Jesus says, "Your will be done, on earth as it is in heaven" (6:10). We see this desire most pronounced in Jesus' own example, in His very mission to do the will of the Father, rather than His own (Jn 6:38). We see it most particularly in His submission to the will of the Father even to the cross: "Nevertheless, not My will, but Yours, be done" (Lk 22:42). He is our supreme example—even for this most difficult prayer—difficult to swallow, and difficult to do, for it takes me away from *me* and directs me to *Him*. So, do I seek God's will, as it is revealed in His Word and through prayer?

PETITION

We come, now, to what we see more naturally as our "prayer requests." They are not what we might tend to ask for. Yet they are truly and simply what we need.

The first is asking for daily *dependence.* As He turns the prayer toward us, Jesus says, "Give us this day our daily bread" (6:11). This, you might say, is all of the "bothersome" cares of this world. But they are not a bother to God. Rather, we are to look to God as our Provider and learn day-by-day dependence upon Him. It is a lesson the children of Israel had to learn early in their desert journey—and that serves as a template for us all in the life of faith (see Ex 16).

Notice, though, that He does not say, "Give us this day our *annual* bread (or our bread for a comfy retirement)," nor does He say, "Give us this day our daily steak and lobster." This is not a prosperity prayer. On the contrary, it is a prayer specifically designed to keep us daily trusting Him. Yes, God is concerned with, and provides for, our welfare. And He desires us to ask of Him what we need to live. But when our prayer becomes, "Lord, make me rich and famous," or "Lord, I could really use that nice new toy," we have begun to stray from the heart of God. As someone has said, "God provides for our 'need' and not for our 'greed.'" But do we trust that He will provide?

This is a hard lesson to learn. Sometimes God keeps us "paycheck to paycheck" or places us in situations of uncertainty, like job loss, etc., to keep us aware of our dependence on Him or to bring us back to that awareness. For we have a tendency even in Christian circles to get so security-focused or future-safety-minded that we lose sight of this fundamental attitude of daily dependence and trust.

The final focus of Jesus' model prayer for us is that of casting ourselves on the *mercy* of God. We see this first when Jesus says, "And forgive us our debts, as we also have forgiven our debtors" (6:12). This is certainly sobering.

On one side, it is a great relief that we can be forgiven—simply by asking the Lord and trusting in Him, that our enormous debt to God can we wiped away. How many of you are living in debt right now: most or all? It is a horrible burden, a form of slavery. We feel its weight and long to be free. Our Lord wants this picture to weigh upon us—but it is so much more.

On the other hand, we are sternly reminded that we cannot presume to come to God for mercy if our hearts are not willing to extend that same mercy to others who have wronged us. This is a small debt compared to our enormous debt before God, as Jesus expands on in 6:14-15, and especially in the parable of the unforgiving servant in Mt 18:21-35. In fact, we need to forgive others first. It is not a matter of *earning* God's forgiveness, which we by no means can; but rather an attitude that recognizes that "a *forgiven* person is a *forgiving* person." If you are unwilling to forgive, then you have not tasted of the grace of God, or you have lost your taste and must regain it through deep repentance.

Finally He says, "And lead us not into temptation, but deliver us from evil" (6:13). This points to our frailty in a fallen world. It reminds us that there is both personal sin and real evil in this world, and we are susceptible to them both, and that "there, but for the grace of God, go I." So we need—and we have—God as our Protector and Deliverer. Let us cast ourselves, therefore, on the mercy of God.

In this supremely well-known and well-loved passage that brings to us the Lord's Prayer, Jesus unwraps for us the basics of prayer. What are they? Do they need to sound spiritual and showy? Do we need to go on and on, or say the right words in the right way? No, not at all. When prayer has simply become religious ritual and is emptied of all meaning, it will fall on deaf ears. God is not interested in religion for show or religion for selfishness. What God is interested in is our very life—and all of it. In prayer, we come close to God in the simple language of a child. Indeed, this is the very picture that Jesus portrays. The basis of our prayer is this tremendous privilege and beautiful relationship to a heavenly Father. Out of that relationship we are to bring to Him in a simple and straightforward manner our praises and petitions. God is pleased both to hear and to answer the requests of His children. What good father would not be?

GOING HUNGRY
ON PURPOSE

(Matthew 6:16-18)

And when you fast, do not look gloomy like the hypocrites,
for they disfigure their faces that their fasting may be seen by others.
Truly, I say to you, they have received their reward.
But when you fast, anoint your head and wash your face,
that your fasting may not be seen by others
but by your Father who is in secret.
And your Father who sees in secret will reward you.

As Christians, we love to gather to *feast* (not that this is bad—in fact, it is a great thing). But do we ever gather to *fast?* Do we even consider it? You might think, "Isn't that a bit weird?" By the way, what a difference one letter can make when it changes the whole picture—from *feast* to *fast,* from getting full to going hungry. We can see something like this in those church bulletin bloopers like, "Potluck supper Sunday at 5:00 pm—prayer and medication to follow" (instead of "medi*t*ation").

Unlike most of the rest of the world, for us to go hungry is something we rarely do—I mean *really* hungry, because it is unpleasant. We might go hungry accidentally because circumstances force us to, or we get too involved in something to break away. But no one would ever go hungry on *purpose*...would they? Why would anyone choose to go without—and be happy about it?

Jesus is addressing a "problem/solution" here. But we may not even see the problem—because, who fasts? In our food-saturated culture, with what seems like a McDonald's on every corner, a Domino's and Taco Bell just down the way, fasting is like an odd-looking stranger that wanders in and you hope quickly wanders out. But strange as it may seem to us, fasting has always been a spiritual pursuit. What is fasting? Simply stated, fasting is abstaining from food for spiritual purposes. It makes a serious statement about longing and need, and about what longing and need must be first. As a spiritual pursuit, then, it is a fundamentally good thing. But like all good things, it can be perverted.[35]

The Problem: Fasting

In this third pillar of Jewish piety in Jesus' day, Jesus identifies the problem as fasting before others. This is the same problem as "religion for show" that Jesus had already addressed with regard to giving and praying.

In the Old Testament, God only *commanded* His people to fast once a year—on the Day of Atonement, that special day of humbling before God because of our sin. This, however, rightly sets a precedent for other occasions of coming before God in times of extreme need or urgency. A notable example is the impending disaster promised by the prophet Joel because of the continued sins of God's people, and the call for community repentance.

> "Yet even now," declares the Lord,
>   "return to Me with all your heart,
> With fasting, with weeping, and with mourning;
>   And rend your hearts and not your garments."
> Who knows whether He will not turn and relent,
>   and leave a blessing behind Him?
> Blow the trumpet in Zion;
>   consecrate a fast;
> call a solemn assembly;
>   gather the people.
> Between the vestibule and the altar
>   let the priests, the ministers of the Lord, weep
> and say, "Spare Your people, O Lord" (Jl 2:12-17).

But by the time of Jesus' day, the Pharisees had taken this action of

---

35 For a key Old Testament example of the perversion of fasting as an external ritual divorced from the demands of genuine piety, and of the Lord's pointed repudiation and redirection, see Isaiah 58.

self-abasement in seeking God and ritualized it. Now they were fasting two days every week (see Lk 18:12). They made sure that everyone knew just how spiritual they were by their gloomy faces, etc.

This is our tendency still, is it not, though not always the fasting issue? We are not immune from this same kind of "religion for show," even without thinking about it. A classic example is the teaching of the early church that is found in the Didache (a religious primer from the first or second century A.D.):

> Let not your fasts be with the hypocrites, for they fast on Mondays and Thursdays, but do you fast on Wednesdays and Fridays (8:1)! [36]

Later generations of Christians often saw this as a litmus test for true piety, and mandated and regulated it, against the spirit of the law as Christ describes it.

But what are our issues? Is it how we give or pray, as Jesus addressed earlier, which are indeed continuing issues for us? Do we pray for the praise of man or the praise of God? Or is it the things we abstain from (as a sign of being a better Christian) or the things we indulge in (as a sign of our freedom in Christ)? You see, "the heart is deceitful above all things" (Jer 17:9), and we are not immune from mixed motives.

And this leads us to God's priorities. What God really wants to see is "religion from the heart." In all their acts of religious devotion, they were "putting the cart before the horse" (to borrow the old adage). They thought that simply doing certain good deeds would prove their merit before God ("Look, God, how religious I am. Look, God, how righteous I am.")—without being concerned with whether they were actually doing these things *for God* (which they were not) or *from faith* (which they were not). These are the heart issues, the big issues, and the issues that must always stay up front. This is like faith and works in relation to our salvation: we have got to keep *faith* in front. So also with our spiritual life, a heart toward God must always lead the way, or it is not pleasing to Him, for "without faith it is impossible to please" God (Heb 11:6).

---

36 Apostolic Fathers, vol. 1, trans. Kirsopp Lake, *Loeb Classical Library*, no. 24, ed. G. P. Goold (Cambridge, MA: Harvard University Press, 1985), 321.

THE SOLUTION: FASTING

Jesus identified the problem, which was fasting before others. Jesus also presents the solution which is fasting before God. Notice that I use the same word for both, because *fasting*, in and of itself, was not the problem. To use an analogy: they were washing the baby in dirty bath water. But you "don't throw the baby out with the bath water." You save the baby and pour new water. We saw it before, you will notice it again: Jesus says "when" and not "if." Jesus assumes the practice of fasting as a function of piety.

In preparation for His earthly ministry (Mt 4:1-4), Jesus Himself went through an extreme period of fasting (forty days and nights), under the temptations of the devil. Through this experience, He understood in a deeper way that "My food is to do the will of Him who sent Me and to accomplish His work" (Jn 4:34), which was ultimately the work of the cross. This is how He was prepared. His priorities were not set on His own needs and desires, but on the desires of His heavenly Father. As He readies Himself in Gethsemane to finally face the cross, He echoes this again: "Not as I will, but as You will" (Mt 26:39).

Fasting also became a part of personal and community times of deep searching and prayers for divine guidance, deliverance, confession, or healing. A notable example in the life of the early church involved the sending out of the first missionaries to the Gentiles.

> Now there were in the church at Antioch prophets and teachers, Barnabas, Simeon who was called Niger, Lucius of Cyrene, Manaen a member of the court of Herod the tetrarch, and Saul. While they were worshiping the Lord *and fasting*, the Holy Spirit said, "Set apart for Me Barnabas and Saul for the work to which I have called them." Then *after fasting* and praying they laid their hands on them and sent them off (Acts 13:1-3).

This is where it hits us: it does not need to be regular and ordinary; but it should be a real and extraordinary means of piety in our lives—both individual and corporate, for self-humbling and deep seeking.

So, how are we to fast? If I can paraphrase Jesus here—keep it spiritual, and keep it secret. By *secret*, I mean you do not want to pretend you are not doing something that you are, but also let it not be showy in any way. The way He describes it, we are to go on our normal way. Anointing and washing (6:17) were normal activities of hygiene, things that people would forego as a signal that they were engaging in this "spiritual" activity. So, when you fast, still take a shower, brush your teeth, wear your normal work clothes, etc. The key is to do it before God and for God alone (even if it is in a group).

And it is to be a *spiritual* act. Some people tout the health benefits of fasting. There may be health benefits, but this should not be the reason we, as Christians, would fast. The same could be said about the intriguing claims of heightened mental clarity and euphoria. On the other hand, there is also something to be said about the health risks of fasting. Thus for some it could be limited in duration or limited in scope—fasting only from all non-liquids perhaps. Again, it is not the ritual itself that is the issue. Fasting is to be a spiritual pursuit. It is going without physical nourishment in order seek spiritual nourishment.

Food is a bodily and regular necessity. If you do not eat, you die. We are whole creatures, our spirit and body are interrelated. So, going for a period of time without normal food intake to seek the Lord is a tangible expression and reminder that we need Him more than food, that "Man shall not live by bread alone, but by every word that comes from the mouth of God" (Mt 4:4). It can serve as a meaningful token of our faith: we seek Him first and more than anything else because our hunger is first for His kingdom and His righteousness (Mt 6:33).

This third chief example of piety is one that may strike us as odd. For who would ever go hungry on purpose? But when we consider the issue of fasting, we need to consider God's intent. It is given to us as a spiritual pursuit. Where do we find our deepest longing and longings fulfilled? Is it in "all these things," or is it in Him? Especially at times of desperate need, or searching, or repentance, it is entirely appropriate, individually or as a church, to set apart a special time for extended prayer and fasting. Whether it becomes a regular course of personal piety is completely up to us, and is to be kept between us and God. But this is a very tangible way to learn to seek Him first, and to find our deepest satisfaction in Him.

15

AMERICAN IDOL

(Matthew 6:19-24)

Do not lay up for yourselves treasures on earth,
where moth and rust destroy and where thieves break in and steal,
but lay up for yourselves treasures in heaven, where neither moth
nor rust destroys and where thieves do not break in and steal.
For where your treasure is, there your heart will be also.
The eye is the lamp of the body.
So, if your eye is healthy, your whole body will be full of light,
but if your eye is bad, your whole body will be full of darkness.
If then the light in you is darkness, how great is the darkness!
No one can serve two masters,
for either he will hate the one and love the other,
or he will be devoted to the one and despise the other.
You cannot serve God and money.

WE do not overtly worship Baal anymore. We recognize that the gods of the nations are false gods and vain hopes. But we still worship idols. Their names have just changed. Now we worship things like money. And as Jesus calls it, God and money are rival gods (6:24). The ancient pagans offered good and precious things—even their infant children—as sacrifices to the gods to get what they wanted. We are not guilty of that, but we still offer sacrifices to our idols. For example, do you sacrifice the needs of your family to get ahead at work? Or do you sacrifice your time with God to spend time with friends? Or do you sacrifice opportunities to do good so that you will have more opportunities to get rich?

Materialism is a rampant problem in our society, and sadly, it exists as well in our churches. It is an ideology that "matter is all that matters," and it is a lifestyle driven by how much I can possess and consume. It is also a focus and a loyalty that stands completely contrary to Christ. So, as we enter this group of verses, we see that Jesus hones in on the issue of our focus and loyalty. He does so in three paragraphs and three analogies that build on one another and reinforce each other. For in this life, there are two chief contenders vying for priority: God and "stuff"—and neither accepts the compromise of a shared devotion.

Where Is My Heart?

The first area of our focus and loyalty is the heart (6:19-21). Where is my heart—in earth or heaven? "For where your treasure is, there your heart will be also" (6:21). We begin with the heart issue again. As we have already seen, the heart of the matter is the matter of the heart. But what Jesus is driving home for us here is that the position of our heart is revealed by the things we treasure. What we focus on, what we pursue, what we prize, is an indication of where our heart is. So, measured by my treasure, where is my heart? Am I seeking the things of God, or just "things" (see 6:33)?

Here, too, we see that our ordinary priorities (money, time, effort, desire) express our spiritual priorities. For example, although it can be overstated, a church budget is a spiritual document; our spending priorities speak to our spiritual priorities. If your church were to allocate only a paltry amount to missions (whether domestic or abroad), what would that say about the spiritual character of the church? We can say we seek the things of God, but if we do not spend time with the Lord or among God's people, or volunteer in ways of service and ministry, how can we say we treasure these things? Our spiritual priorities are revealed in our day-to-day lives by what we prize and pursue.

So, let us look at this more closely and contrast, as Jesus does here, an earthward focus and a heavenward focus. There are certain key and obvious *indicators* of an earthward focus. We see it in phrases like: "I want what I want, and I want it now" (instant gratification); "keeping up with the Joneses"; or "the one who dies with the most toys wins." Yet we all know that the one who dies with the most toys...still dies; and you can not take it with you. This is our society in a nutshell, is it not? We grasp, we want, we are obsessed with stuff. We want the best for ourselves or the best for our children. But it is all self- or stuff-centered.

Where is the desire for goodness, and for the fame and reputation of the gospel? Where is the desire first to trust in God, repent of sin, and strive for righteousness? Where is the desire to see Christ in-dwelling us and our children?

There are some innate and glaring *frustrations* of an earthward focus as well. The refrain of Ecclesiastes brings this out strongly: "Vanity of vanities! All is vanity" (Eccl 1:2)—a vapor (*poof*), empty, transient, meaningless. What does it matter? Everything fades and everyone dies. In our modern society that has everything, we still struggle with this same ancient call. One thing we learn better as we grow older is that everything wears out— including us. And though we have it all, we find ourselves always wanting more, and yet are never satisfied. And what is more, without an eternal perspective to govern, this "aha!" moment of "what does it matter?" leads to all sorts of destructive "isms"—nihilism (why live?), hedonism (live for self and pleasure), and despotism (live for power and dominance).

Or as Jesus says it here: this is "where moth and rust destroy and where thieves break in and steal" (6:19). Cars naturally break down or get wrecked; wax moths naturally destroy perfectly good honeycomb (a frustration when I was a beekeeper); the stock market can rise or plummet; relationships can come to an end. We purchase insurance; we set up alarm systems. We seek security against all these things, though we can never really guarantee it. But God does... in heaven. Everything there such as goodness, beauty, people is eternally secure.

Some people claim that "if you are too heavenly minded, you will be no earthly good." But that is not the case, if it is properly understood. Looking out for others more than yourself; wanting to see others freed from the fear of death, the bondage of sin, and the burden of guilt; giving assistance to the needy, and even being kind to your enemies—these are some of the things that flow from a heavenly mind. They are heaven's treasure, which shows itself in a life not consumed with worry and woes, but with peace and joy! Take a look around at those who set their hearts on heaven. You will see both the difference it makes in their own lives and the difference it makes in the lives of others—because they are living for things that are bigger and better.

So then, we should ask ourselves: Where is my heart? Where is my treasure? What do I prize and pursue?

HOW IS MY EYESIGHT?

The second focus and loyalty is revealed by our eyes (6:22-23). How is my eyesight: blind or clear? Many of you who are reading this currently wear glasses or contacts, or have had some form of corrective eye surgery. Do you remember what life was like before that, and the difference that clear vision makes, especially before and after cataract surgery? For my own case, I did not even know I needed glasses until I was in Junior High. I just thought that things were supposed to look blurry at a distance! Then one Sunday, we were looking at the park across from the church, and at the blurry leaves on the chestnut trees, and one of my friends handed me his glasses. I put them on and—wow!—the leaves all of a sudden became clear and defined. What a difference clear vision makes!

Blurry vision is bad enough, but do you know any blind people? What do you notice about them? You see them having to be very careful and tentative, led along with a walking stick or a seeing-eye dog. You see, our eyesight matters. The eyes are what guide us. As Jesus says, they are "the lamp of the body" (6:22); and it is through them that the rest of our life is filled either with light or with darkness, literally and figuratively. Where our gaze is set makes all the difference in the course and outlook of our whole life. Picking up from the heart, which sets the stage: if our vision is heavenly focused, our life will be *alive;* but if our vision is stuck here, it is like living blind. By the way, the "healthy" eye (in 6:22) is literally "single" (ἁπλοῦς). Jesus is calling us to a single, clear, and proper focus on God, on the things of God, with a heart, mind, and will toward God. Is that where your vision is set? It makes all the difference.

There is a danger here of self-deception. It is a very real danger, and it would be very bad. Jesus briefly addresses it in these enigmatic words: "If then the light in you is darkness, how great is the darkness!" (6:23). That is, there are people who think they are light inside—that they are good people, and good before God—but they really do not have their focus on God and heaven, as God shows it to us. Their focus remains on themselves and the stuff of this earth. Jesus says that the darkness here is very great.

Often it is the good and religious people that are the blindest ones of all—because they think they see (see Jn 9:40-41). Do you know people (or perhaps are you one of them) who think they are good or religious, and because of that they think they will go to heaven? At how many funerals do you hear that "so-and-so is in a better place now because he was a good man." Very few people, who believe there is a heaven, will tell you that they think they are going to hell. They will say that hell is only for the *really* bad people—as if God grades on the curve, and not on an absolute standard that would damn us all, except for His grace (recall Mt 5:20).

Even genuine Christians are not immune; for we can be deceived into thinking we are not as bad as we are, that we do not need to really repent, that sin is not the issue, that it is something else, or someone else. A lot of counseling skirts around this issue, and a lot of popular preaching ignores this very issue. People's lives are not transformed, because they have not seen the darkness of their own sin and the light of God's grace. Or sin gets redefined, so that I can do what I want and still claim to follow God. But the apostle John tells us (in a threefold sequence): "If we say we have fellowship with Him while we walk in darkness, we lie"; and "If we say we have no sin, we deceive ourselves"; and "If we say we have not sinned, we make Him a liar" (1 Jn 1:6, 8, 10). We can never graduate out of repentance; we always need to turn back to the light with open eyes and open heart.

Who Is My Master?

The third and final focus is the loyalty itself (6:24). Who is my master: greed or God?

In this third group of verses, we notice that there is an underlying description of the progression of sin from inclination to action, from *heart* to *blindness* to *slavery*. This is how sin works in each of our lives: it *begins* in the heart, then *blinds* the mind, and then *binds* the will. Do not be fooled; sin is not to be toyed with. It reminds us, too, that we need to constantly address and be constantly vigilant about the issue of sin at the level of the heart, facing it before we find ourselves blinded by and to its negative influence and then bound in its destructive control.

Whether we like it or not, we are all slaves to something or someone. As Bob Dylan[37] so frankly put it: "Well, it may be the devil or it may be the Lord, but you're gonna have to serve somebody." Or as Jesus sets it out

---

37 Gotta Serve Somebody. Written by Bob Dylan. Copyright © 1979 Special Rider Music. All rights reserved. International copyright secured. Reprinted by permission.

here: it is either God or money. You can only call one of them "Master." We like to think that we can love both—even serve both. In fact, that is how much of the American church lives. But Jesus demands an undivided loyalty. Only one thing can be first in our lives.

But why does Jesus pick on money here? Literally, it is "mammon," which is the Aramaic word for wealth or possessions. What is so vicious about that? Essentially, it is a neutral thing, and it is often considered a blessing from the Lord. *But* it is a blessing that can easily become corrupted if our affections become attached to the gifts rather than to the Giver. We see, in our affluent culture, how it leads us deceptively away from God: there is no longer any felt need for Him. But a "need for God" is where we *all* must begin and *always* must stay (recall Mt 5:3). God has, thus, been effectively replaced by mammon: money and stuff. That is why, in Jesus' mind, God and money are rival gods. Or, as the Scriptures elsewhere make it crystal clear: *Greed is idolatry* (Col 3:5). Jesus will later comment on how hard it is for a rich man to enter heaven (Mt 19:23-24). Do we take that seriously—in our own pursuit of possessions?

The apostle Paul similarly says:

> Those who desire to be rich fall into temptation, into a snare, into many senseless and harmful desires that plunge people into ruin and destruction. For the love of money is a root of all kinds of evils. It is through this craving that some have wandered away from the faith and pierced themselves with many pangs (1 Tm 6:9-10).

The love of money is a false god. Unfortunately this idolatry of mammon is increasingly our American idol. For anything we love *more* than Jesus has become our idol. And God has said, as the first of His commands: "You shall have no other gods before Me" (Ex 20:3).

Where do we see this idolatry in our own lives? Pull out a dollar bill from your wallet or purse and take a look at it. What does all our money proclaim? "In God we trust" and it is a fitting reminder. But the American system runs on the rule, "In money we trust." To take an extreme example, if left with the choice to give up everything you own or to give up God, which would you choose? Or to lower your standard of living to serve God in some way, which would you choose?

We might tend to think that this is an idol for rich grown-ups, and we certainly see it there. But we could just as well be a kid and poor and still have this as our idol—and it usually is. Here are some questions to consider: Where is your heart? What drives you? What do you prize and pursue? Do you strive to be rich or do you strive to be godly? Do you envy the prosperous and carefree or do you yearn for God's presence (see Ps 73)? When the pursuit of wealth or stuff and time to spend on your pleasures, and the pursuit of God come into conflict, as they will often do, who wins out in your life? Say, for instance, you stay up late partying on Saturday night, so you sleep in on Sunday and miss church; or you are always so busy doing something that you cannot stop and seek the Lord in prayer or in His Word. Who wins out? Whom do we serve? And how do we fight our attraction toward this rival master?

FIRST, we fight at the level of attitude. What is one of the first lessons we have to teach our children? To share. "But it is mine. I earned it; I get to keep it." We continue to say this as adults, do we not? But this was a lesson the early church learned well.

> Now the full number of those who believed were of one heart and soul, and no one said that any of the things that belonged to him was his own, but they had everything in common. And with great power the apostles were giving their testimony to the resurrection of the Lord Jesus, and great grace was upon them all. There was not a needy person among them, for as many as were owners of lands or houses sold them and brought the proceeds of what was sold and laid it at the apostles' feet, and it was distributed to each as any had need (Acts 4:32-35).

This was not being leveled out; it was an intentional use of their stuff to meet the needs of others. We need to view our money and things not as somehow deserved or ours to do with as we like, but rather as blessings *from* God and to be used *for* God. In the church I pastor, we characteristically sing the Doxology right after receiving the tithes and offerings. It is this very good reminder: "Praise God from whom all blessings flow."

SECOND, strive at the level of action. Generosity is the best way to counteract greed. Notice how Paul counseled the wealthy people in young Pastor Timothy's church:

> As for the rich in this present age, charge them not to be haughty, nor to set their hopes on the uncertainty of riches, but on God, who richly provides us with everything to enjoy. They are to do good, to be rich in good works, to be generous and ready to share, thus storing up treasure for themselves as a good foundation for the future, so that they may take hold of that which is truly life (1 Tm 6:17-19).

In pointing them to God, he redirects their riches and the focus of their treasure. So, do you walk around with a closed fist or an open hand?

Hear again the threefold question: Where is my heart? How is my vision? Whom do I serve? As Jesus says, God and money are rival gods. It is impossible to claim to live for Christ if your life is motivated by greed—by the pursuit of money and all the things that money can buy, even friends and fame and so on. This is like what we have seen on several seasons of "American Idol." America, this is your idol, and it is also the idol of some American churches. Which will you choose?

16

ANXIETY DISORDER

(Matthew 6:25-34)

Therefore I tell you, do not be anxious about your life,
what you will eat or what you will drink,
nor about your body, what you will put on.
Is not life more than food, and the body more than clothing?
Look at the birds of the air: they neither sow nor reap
nor gather into barns, and yet your heavenly Father feeds them.
Are you not of more value than they?
And which of you by being anxious
can add a single hour to his span of life?
And why are you anxious about clothing? Consider the lilies
of the field, how they grow: they neither toil nor spin, yet I tell you,
even Solomon in all his glory was not arrayed like one of these.
But if God so clothes the grass of the field,
which today is alive and tomorrow is thrown into the oven,
will He not much more clothe you, O you of little faith?
Therefore do not be anxious, saying, "What shall we eat?"
or "What shall we drink?" or "What shall we wear?"
For the Gentiles seek after all these things,
and your heavenly Father knows that you need them all.
But seek first the kingdom of God and His righteousness,
and all these things will be added to you.
Therefore do not be anxious about tomorrow,
for tomorrow will be anxious for itself.
Sufficient for the day is its own trouble.

ANXIETY disorders are a *huge* problem in our current society. According to the statistics, *nineteen million* Americans suffer from some form of anxiety disorder—like panic attacks, phobias, and so on—and over seven million receive medication to assuage the symptoms. Jesus tackles this huge problem head-on...but not in the way you might think.

There is a typical routine whenever you enter the doctor's office: you come in with certain symptoms, and from those symptoms the doctor seeks to diagnose what the real problem is and then prescribe a treatment for it. Like any good doctor, Jesus is not here just to soften the symptom. Instead, He uncovers the root cause and prescribes the remedy. The symptom is anxiety. The root cause is unbelief. The treatment is: "seek *first* the kingdom of God" (6:32), not "all these things."

THE SYMPTOM: ANXIETY

Worry is certainly *the glaring issue in this section.* Six times we see this repetition of being "anxious" (in verses 25, 27, 28, 31, and twice in verse 34). As the old saying goes: "Repetition is the key to learning." Here, it is repeated for emphasis.

Just in case we missed it, there is a threefold "therefore" as well, and it is tied to the command, "Do not be anxious" (6:25, 31, 34). It has been commonly stated, and rightly so, that we need to ask: "What is the 'therefore' 'there for'?" As we found out in the last chapter, money and the pursuit of it is a rival god (6:24). Greed and a focus on the things of this earth more than on the things of God, are nothing less than blatant idolatry. They are increasingly, in fact, our American idols. Therefore we are continuing to examine how Jesus speaks to the issue of idolatry in our lives, which manifests itself not only in the things we prize but also in our obsessions.

Worry is also *a glaring issue in our society,* even in people that have everything. We worry about our health, our weight, our finances, our relationships ("she loves me, she loves me not"). We are obsessed with our appearance—our beauty or the age we look and what people will think. Billions are spent on creams and colors and cosmetic surgeries. Among the things that Jesus brings out here is that we worry about what clothes to wear, although He was probably thinking more about just *having* clothes rather than having the right ones. And He speaks to our worry about how to add to the length of our life; but do we bother to ask ourselves whether our time is well spent? Anxiety is my personal tendency, as my mom will readily admit, since I got the "worry gene" from her. A care-free attitude does not come naturally to me. And yet, anxiety is a symptom at some level or other that we all see and that we all face.

But worry does no good. It is a hard master that demands everything and yet gives nothing in return. As Jesus observes, it cannot change anything—even add a single hour to your life (6:27). It is the way of the world—but not of a believer. We have something better: a heavenly Father (6:32). Worry always tends to borrow from itself—with interest (6:34). A popular song by Bobby McFerrin says it well: "In your life expect some trouble, but when you worry you make it double. Don't worry, be happy."[38]

THE DIAGNOSIS: UNBELIEF

The medical diagnosis of any malady depends on uncovering the root cause, to find out what is manifesting the troubling symptom, in order to determine what is really wrong with you. Not like the humorous anecdote about a lady who came to the doctor and said (moving her shoulder socket), "It hurts when I do this." To which the doctor curtly replied, "Well, stop doing that." Here, the symptom is anxiety, a persistent worry which hits so many of us and is all-consuming for some. What is the root cause? For Jesus, it is merely a matter of *stating the obvious.*

He begins by opening our eyes to the obvious all *around* us. Jesus as the master teacher uses the power of picture; and looking up and looking down, He directs us to the birds of the air and the lilies of the field. Here He argues from the lesser to the greater, a common and effective argument, showing us that we have no reason to be anxious about the things of this life. God feeds the birds, and yet we are of *more* value than they (6:26). God clothes the grass, so how much *more* will He take care of us (6:30)? God provides for both of them, but He is so much *more* to us: He is our heavenly Father.

Here are a couple of caveats: This is not meant to encourage idleness or to discourage a responsible concern for the provision of legitimate needs. Even the birds have to look for their food, but the key is that it is there to be found. We, in like manner, are to live in expectant reliance on the power and care of God—not for our wants but for our needs, or as Jesus called it earlier our "daily bread" (6:11). God's provision for our

---

38 "Don't Worry, Be Happy" by Bobby McFerrin, from his album *Simple Pleasures.* Best Song Grammy 1989. Probnoblem Music. All rights reserved. Used by permission.

needs does not guarantee a life that is free of trouble. But He knows both the needs of today *and* tomorrow. As in the saying, "We will cross that bridge when we come to it," He can be trusted to handle our needs when the time comes.

When Jesus comes to the heart of the passage, He opens our eyes to the obvious *within* us, and He says, "O you of little faith" (6:30). Here, Jesus hits the nail on the head: He diagnoses the disease. It is certainly not what we *want* to hear, nor what we *think* the problem is. However, He is right that it is the problem of "practical unbelief"—not what we know, but how we live by a fundamental lack of faith. There are two aspects to this, picking up on the illustrations He just used:

First, worry betrays a lack of faith in *who God is to us* as our "heavenly Father" (6:26, 32). Notice that when Jesus uses God's care for the birds as an illustration for us, He does not call God "their" heavenly Father; He calls Him "your" heavenly Father (meaning, ours). You see, God does not have that special relationship with the rest of His creation—and yet He cares for them. How much more will He care for us, who are His own dear children? And a good father always wants good things for his children (as we will see in Mt 7:9-11).

Second, worry betrays a lack of faith in *how valuable we are to God* (6:26). Where do you place your value? What makes you feel special or important, or the opposite, insignificant? Is it how much you earn, or what you can or cannot do? The world judges our worth on such things as our education or potential, special talents, or our earning power. But God does not calculate our value by these things. We are valuable to God simply because we are His.

Those of you who are parents: How valuable are your children to you? Are they valuable because of their abilities, or are they valuable simply because they are your children and you love them? So it is with us. We have a heavenly Father who loves us and has chosen us to be in a special relationship with Him. That gives us worth beyond count or comparison! I am valuable to the God of the universe, who sent His only Son to die for me so that I might live with Him. Do you see your value there? Do not settle for the fickleness of the world nor for its applause or its rejection.

But do I trust Him? This is the question that comes back to each of us. Do I trust Him to take care of my needs, to watch over my family, to do what is right, even when so much can go wrong, or even looks wrong? Do I trust Him? This is where the rubber meets the road and it is revealed in a life either of peace or of anxiety. Worry and stress are the way of the world; but peace is the way of Christ. Jesus said: "Peace I leave with you; My peace I give to you. Not as the world gives do I give to you" (Jn 14:27). Do you want that peace? Do you want to give up your anxious cares? He will show you how. And He will take them.

THE TREATMENT: "SEEK FIRST"

We come now to the course of treatment: "Seek first." This, again, is the issue of focus, of drive, of devotion (versus idolatry). Two ways are placed before us that reveal a contrast in *seeking* (6:32-33).

The worldly (Gentiles) *seek* "all these things" (6:32). But a devotion and focus on the stuff of this earth leads only to enslavement, as here, the enslavement to anxiety. For who is left in control of your cares, if everything is *here?* You are, and you cannot keep away the moth and the thief forever (see 6:19-20). Are you living in this prison of fear and worry, consumed with always needing something more *here*, or seeking something or someone to be secure *here?* These fears may look like "the life." But You can be free! In your soul, you know that there is something better, and that is freedom and peace. And you know that there is someone else who is much bigger. *God is in control, and He cares for you!*

But Jesus says *we are to seek* something else; that we must *seek first* something completely different, and all the rest will follow. That is, the Lord will provide for what you need or what is ultimately best because He is a good Father. It is a drastic change in focus, drive, and devotion. He says: "Seek first the kingdom of God and His righteousness" (6:33). This must be our first priority: not "things first" but "*first* things first." All else must be secondary, including our desires, dreams, goals, careers, and even our families. God must always take first place in all things because only He is God.

So then, what does it mean to seek His kingdom and righteousness? Simply, it is another way of saying "seek the will and the way of God." This kind of seeking takes conscious effort. "Seeking" Him does not just happen, since we naturally default to "self." Seeking is an active striving for something. So, are you doing this?

By definition, His kingdom refers to the territory and people subject to His rulership. If you belong to Him, then He rules over you and over all that you might consider your "space." It is not yours—*you* are not yours; it is all His. If He is my King (and He is a kind King), then I must submit to His will in all of my life. There is no space that is *mine* (see 1 Cor 6:19-20).

His righteousness is His character and His commands that are all good and all "right." Where is His righteousness found? In the Bible. So, are you reading the Bible—first to know and then to follow in His way—in your day-to-day life? In each and every circumstance, is it your instinct to think and to ask: Will this promote the honor of God—or my honor? Will this make Jesus look good—or myself? Asking "What would Jesus have me do?" is not a bad way to begin.

We are tested in all ways and in every weighty decision, but some of you reading this right now are undoubtedly having to wrestle with the natural anxiety of current or looming unemployment. How will the Lord guide and provide for me and my family next? Or with the turn in the economy, how will I continue to make ends meet?

Will I live under the dominion of worry, in service to the idolatry of "all these things"? Or will I place my trust in my heavenly Father's care, knowing that He cares for me, and so put my priorities first where they first must be? Jesus prescribes our constant remedy: "Seek first the kingdom of God and His righteousness, and all these things will be added to you" (6:33).

WHO ARE YOU TO JUDGE?

(Matthew 7:1-6)

Judge not, that you be not judged.
For with the judgment you pronounce you will be judged,
and with the measure you use it will be measured to you.
Why do you see the speck that is in your brother's eye,
but do not notice the log that is in your own eye?
Or how can you say to your brother, "Let me take the speck
out of your eye," when there is the log in your own eye?
You hypocrite, first take the log out of your own eye, and then
you will see clearly to take the speck out of your brother's eye.
Do not give dogs what is holy, and do not throw your pearls before
pigs, lest they trample them underfoot and turn to attack you.

JUST days before the election in November, 2006, we were at first disturbed by the allegations against Ted Haggard, and then deeply saddened and disappointed when they proved to be at least partly true. Here he was, a star of evangelicalism: current president of the National Association of Evangelicals, personal friend of Dr. James Dobson, in periodic contact with the President of the United States, senior pastor of the vibrant 14,000 member New Life Church in Colorado Springs, and champion of such grand moral issues as heterosexual marriage. Yet there was a dark side to his life, that he had evidently struggled with for some time, which was exposed when Mike Jones, a gay male prostitute, stepped forward and "outed" him. Was it politically motivated? Yes, admittedly so—by Jones himself. It was because a proposed amendment banning same-sex marriage was on the ballot for November 7. But the key issue that was placed at the top was the looming "h" word: hypocrisy. As Jones told ABC news: "I had to expose the hypocrisy. He is in a position of influence [for] millions of followers, and he is preaching against gay marriage. But behind everybody's back [he is] doing what he has preached against."

So the name of Christ is shamed and the cause of Christ is ridiculed. If you followed the flurry of blogging surrounding this incident, the vitriol was quite intense. And out of things like that, Christians are often and rightly asked: "Who are you to judge?" And there are deep wounds to be healed and deep sins to be dealt with. Will we, the church, learn once again to humble ourselves in the sight of the Lord (Jas 4:10)?

As we enter this next section of His sermon (7:1-12, capped by the Golden Rule), Jesus turns to the issue of right judgment. Haggard had been making judgments against homosexuality. Then Jones shot back with judgments against hypocrisy. Everyone makes judgments, but they are just basing them on different standards. How do we get a handle on it? Jesus addresses this issue of judgment at its most basic level.

ERR ON THE SIDE OF GRACE

The basic teaching that Jesus outlines in the first two verses is this: Do not be *so* judgmental! But let us flesh out this basic teaching by way of two questions.

First, the question of meaning. When Jesus issued those stark words, "Judge not" (7:1), He set a blaze that continues to our day. What does He mean by this? Does He mean *do not judge at all*?

There are a few verses of Scripture that non-Christians—and especially, anti-Christians—love to quote, usually yanked out of context, and this is one of them. When confronted with a value statement that "such-and-such a practice is wrong," they are quick to quote Jesus' words, "Judge not, that you be not judged" (7:1), as a slam-dunk way to avoid the issue and justify their sinful lifestyle. Or they might retort: "Are you perfect?" with the obvious and universal answer, "No." "Then who are *you* to judge?" So is this what Jesus means, that we are not to judge at all?

It cannot mean that, for even in this very context Jesus Himself refers to some people as *hypocrites* (7:5) and others as (gasp!) *dogs* and *pigs* (7:6). These are certainly judgments! And elsewhere, Jesus calls us *to* "judge with right judgment" (John 7:24).

So, the issue is not judgment in general—which includes discernment and distinguishing between good and evil or better and worse, which we are called to do. It is rather some *kind* of judgment that is explained by the context, for, as in all things, context is key.

Rather, the issue here is one of not being (in our sense of the word) *judgmental*—that is, having an attitude that is quick to pass judgment and to look down on others. This is an attitude that is strictly forbidden for all who would claim to follow Christ. It is here—perhaps in part because of our pursuit of perfection[39]—that we, who claim to follow Christ, so often fail. And we fail, to the mockery of many in the world, although they are usually just as guilty, because judgmentalism is a *human* issue with which we all must struggle. But again, the root, is "self." And religious self-centeredness is still *self*-centered, not *Christ*-centered. That root must be cut out with sharp words. And so Jesus says it sharply: "Judge not!" (7:1).

Second, the question of measure. This issue of a judgmental attitude is made clear by the words that directly follow: "For with the judgment you pronounce you will be judged, and with the measure you use it will be measured to you" (7:2).

Notice that Jesus does not say *who* it is that will judge us: will it be others? or will it be God? The answer probably is: "Yes." It is not a threat; it is a rule. We will be judged, whether by God or by others, by the same standard we use to judge others; we will be treated, whether by God or by others, in the same way or with the same attitude, that we treat others. The way the Golden Rule (in Mt 7:12) is paraphrased: *treat others the way you want to be treated*, is stated here from the other angle: *the way you treat others is the way you will be treated*."

This is the law of sowing and reaping: "Whatever one sows, that will he also reap" (Gal 6:7). If you sow blessing or kindness, you will reap blessing; but if you sow cursing or unkindness, you will reap cursing. To put it crassly: *What goes around comes around*. Or, as another maxim makes specific, *He who would have friends must show himself friendly* (see Prv 18:24a, KJV). So, how do you want others to judge you? Above all, how do you want *God* to judge you (see Mt 6:14-15)?

What a difference the measure makes! How many of you know what it is like to live with a constant cloud of judgment hanging over your

---

39 See Mt 5:48, although the perfection there is the perfection of "love."

head? It is stifling, depressing. But what about a cloud of grace instead? For from grace there is liberty, life, and love. So I ask: Will the measure we use toward others be demeaning and nit-picky, or will it be grace? As my dad rightly taught me on this issue of measure—judgment or grace: If you are going to err, err on the side of grace (or *mercy*; see Jas 2:13).[40]

What does this look like? First, we must be careful to judge only on matters of sin on which God has clearly spoken, and not to judge the motives of the heart, for that is God's jurisdiction. But also, will you judge others on a standard of dress or decorum, on past failures or present struggles; or will you judge only on what really matters? Is that person seeking the Lord (Mt 6:33)? Has that person made progress in the Lord? Is that person showing a desire and taking steps to love, to be responsible, etc.? Encourage those things; for we are called to build each other up, not to tear each other down (see 1 Thes 5:11).[41]

MAKING JUDGMENT CALLS

But also, as Jesus explores in the verses that follow: Do not be *non-judgmental!* By this I do not mean to undo all that I have already said, but to show the balance that Jesus Himself seeks to bring. For our lives are to be characterized by "judge not" (7:1). Yet there are two judgments that Jesus Himself speaks of here.

One, the judgment toward ourselves and sin (7:3-5). As the saying goes, "A picture is worth a thousand words." Jesus, in but a few words, paints a picture that makes the issue oh-so-clear. What we might not see or want to own up to, we do here: this is Exhibit A, the log and the speck. It would be humorous if it were not so sad and so much what we, by nature, do. For the deceitfulness of sin is this: I can be blind to the log in my own eye!

At a saw-mill, two things you will see are mounds of sawdust and piles of logs. Both are wood; but each log is huge and the sawdust particles are just specks. So it is with the illustration here. Both issues are "sin"—log and speck—and we are to see them as sin and seek to take them out. The problem comes when we see that sin in someone else's life, and say

---

40 Compare also, for example, Matthew 9:10-13 and John 8:3-11.

41 Compare also 1 Corinthians 8:1-13 and 10:23-24, along with Hebrews 10:24-25.

"here, let me point it out to you, let me take it out," without some serious self-examination first, and a heart of repentance.

Often the sins we notice most readily in others are the sins we ourselves commit. It is the blight of hypocrisy, in stark relief, when you seek to rid someone else of a small sin, while you yourself are committing that same sin or a much more grievous one. I would point you to the parable and response in 2 Samuel 12:1-7. Again, with the scandal I mentioned, as in previous religious scandals, it is this very hypocrisy, not sin in general, that has once again brought such ridicule on the name of Christ.

This, then, is the call to humility. Humility is recognizing that we all stand as sinners in the sight of God. Thus we confront one another as one sinner to another with the offer of the grace of Christ. It is not wrong, indeed, it is admirable, to seek to aid one's brother or sister in removing sin, even a small sin, from their lives. But *first and foremost*, it is incumbent upon us to examine our own lives to make sure we are free from that sin ourselves or are at least dealing with it, and then that we rebuke and restore only with all gentleness and humility (Gal 6:1). To borrow the language of James 1:19 (in inverted order): Let everyone be slow to rebuke, quick to encourage, quick to self-examine.

Two, the judgment toward *dogs* and *pigs* (7:6), or you could call it judgment on hardness of heart. It is a call to discernment; for we must recognize that there are indeed "dogs and pigs" in this world. There are some who are viciously hardened in their rejection of the grace of God. In the ancient world, dogs were not cuddly and cute or "man's best friend," they were vicious scavengers. Indeed, the Jewish term of contempt for a Gentile (people "without the law") was "dog"; and to the Jews, pigs were the epitomé of the unclean. Yet, ironically, the Jews were sometimes the ones who became viciously hardened in their rejection of the grace of God (Acts 18:5-6), and even some of those within the church "turn back from the holy commandment" and lead in heresy and immorality (2 Pt 2:21-22).

Lack of discernment in this area is seen, for example, in the widespread opinion that we can reason with terrorists, give them some concessions, and they will stop attacking. But apart from a miracle of God's grace, this will never happen: they are (in Jesus' own words) "dogs and pigs"; they will simply turn and tear you apart.

This also affects how we view our task of evangelism, for there will be some who are hardened against the gospel, so that pressing them toward the gospel against their will will not only be fruitless, it will be counter-productive, turning them off in a further and fiercer way. We are to be bold with the gospel, yes, but not obnoxious. Part of this discernment is the knowledge that God remains sovereign in salvation. We are called to be the vessels of His grace. Ultimately, though, it is His work, not ours. Jesus said, "The Son can do…only what He sees the Father doing. For whatever the Father does, that the Son does likewise" (Jn 5:19). So, let us look for areas where the Lord might already be working and step in; let us look for a door that the Lord might already be cracking open and walk through it, because we bear what is most holy and precious—the gospel of God's grace.

As Christians, we are indeed admonished to make "judgment calls," not to discriminate against race or gender, but to distinguish between good versus evil and what is precious versus what is worthless. We have been both pressured and seduced away from this, even to the point of turning these things upside-down. But God says, "Woe to those who call evil good and good evil" (Is 5:20). Yet, even these judgment calls have to be kept under the umbrella of "judge not." We must use discernment, yes, but discernment with great humility—as fellow sinners saved by grace, in need of grace, and called to live in grace. For *grace* is to be the measure that we use.

18

PRAYING WITH CONFIDENCE

(Matthew 7:7-11)

Ask, and it will be given to you; seek, and you will find;
knock, and it will be opened to you.
For everyone who asks receives, and the one who seeks finds,
and to the one who knocks it will be opened.
Or which one of you, if his son asks him for bread, will give him a stone?
Or if he asks for a fish, will give him a serpent?
If you then, who are evil, know how to give good gifts to your children,
how much more will your Father who is in heaven
give good things to those who ask Him!

PRAYER is one of the most precious privileges of the Christian life. But perhaps you do not think so, or perhaps your life does not look as though this is true. Let me ask: Do you find yourself just "naturally" praying throughout the day, as an instinctual response to your day-to-day needs or concerns? In other words, do you acknowledge Him "in all your ways" (as Proverbs 3:6 tells us to)? If not, why not? Is it because you do not believe in it? But prayer is one of those things that clearly separates believers from unbelievers. Or is it because you do not want to bother God, or wonder if He is really listening and really cares about you? Or perhaps you have sinned so badly you fear the Lord will not receive you? Or is it because God is *so sovereign* that it will not make a difference anyway? Are any of those your ideas about prayer?

Or is prayer simply words that you might say before meals or before bed—or even during church, words that sound religious but that you do not really mean? Even our culture still finds it "nice" to pray at official occasions, as long as you do not express any real convictions about any real issues and do not end the prayer "in Jesus' name." Or is it more like speaking good thoughts into the air? Is this your idea about prayer?

I will say it again: prayer is one of the most precious privileges of the Christian life. Jesus certainly thinks so—both in what He preached and what He practiced. When Jesus addresses the issue of prayer for us again, He does not give us a pattern and lay out the basics of prayer, as He did in Matthew 6:9-13 with the Lord's Prayer. Rather here, He speaks to our attitude or approach to God Himself as we come to Him in prayer. And Jesus tells us here that we can pray with confidence, and gives us two clear reasons why.

EXPECT AN ANSWER

THE FIRST REASON is *because Jesus calls us to pray.* Jesus Himself gives us the summons to come and the confidence to receive (7:7-8). But notice here what Jesus does and does not say. He *does not* say: "Wait, hold back, take a passive approach…and you *might* receive, *maybe* you will find, *perhaps* it will be opened." No, He first uses what are three distinctly action and expectant words: "Ask…seek…knock." Then He follows all three with a statement of clear assurance: "And it *will* be given to you," "You *will* find," and "It *will* be opened to you" (7:7). Then, just in case we missed it, He repeats it all in the next verse to underscore this very issue.

And there is a level of persistence that is added as well. In the Greek, these are all present imperatives, that render the nuance: *keep on* asking, *keep on* seeking, *keep on* knocking. This is not something Jesus envisions as being done timidly and periodically, but, rather, boldly and perpetually. This is to be a part of our *life* with God: we are called to "pray without ceasing" (1 Thes 5:17), to "always pray and not give up" (Lk 18:1, NIV).

Thus, there is no stronger way of saying: "Come, keep coming, and keep coming with confidence!" But do we? Is this our attitude in prayer? Too often we (myself included) are hesitant to pray boldly, specifically, expectantly, for something to take place. Sometimes this is because we have become discouraged when God has not answered, maybe over and over. Or perhaps we have even lost faith. We know we should pray, so we do. But we find ourselves praying half-heartedly, without really expecting an answer anymore. What does Jesus say to you? Hear His words again—even in your "disconnect."

Sometimes it is because we have gotten distracted by the need to sound "religious"—where we say a lot of nice and holy things, but we do not really ask for anything specific. Or we pray, and yet always hedge things so that we do not seem too bold. So we bow out of any real conversation or engagement with God. We have come to think that we should not talk to God like that—as you might hear a child do (the *audacity*), and yet that is so often our model, even here. I will point you to one fairly recent example in my own family's life. While our grandbaby Hope was staying with us, she bumped her head very hard, so that there was a big goose-egg and much crying. My wife Lorri told her she could pray to God to make her feel better. She scurried off, as she often does. Then Lorri overheard her as she was lying on the floor with folded hands, praying, "Dear God, please make me better. Thank you. Amen." And you know what? God did; He answered that little girl's prayer. The swelling went completely down without leaving a bruise. And she told us, "Jesus made me better."

So it is here: Jesus calls us to pray boldly, to ask specifically, and to wait expectantly for Him to answer. This is the pattern we see throughout the Scriptures. One prominent example that is set forward for us to follow is that of the "super-prophet" Elijah. Yet it was presented in the context of the ordinary circumstances of praying for healing from sickness and sin.

> Therefore, confess your sins to one another and pray for one
> another, that you may be healed. The prayer of a righteous
> person has great power as it is working. Elijah was a man with
> a nature like ours, and he prayed fervently that it might not
> rain, and for three years and six months it did not rain on
> the earth. Then he prayed again, and heaven gave rain, and
> the earth bore its fruit (Jas 5:16-18).

What do we see here? We see that (1) Elijah was *a man* (that is, one simple prayer from one simple man, woman, or child will do); (2) He had *a nature like ours* (that is, if he could do it, so can we; you do not have to be some "super-saint"); (3) He was a *righteous* person (not "perfect," but a believer, in a right relationship with God, relying on His grace); and (4) he prayed *fervently* (and this fervency is a matter of the heart, not the words). Indeed, Elijah prayed seven times for the return of the rain, and he prayed expectantly each time (see 1 Kgs 18:42-44). Such a prayer from such a person God honors with *great power*. This is what is available for you and for me, when we simply "ask...seek...knock" on heaven's door that opens to our heavenly Father.

AN IMPORTANT PICTURE

THE SECOND REASON we can pray with confidence is *because we have a good Father*. We see this described in Matthew 7:9-11.

What is your picture of God as you approach Him in prayer? Is He distant, unapproachable, like a policeman or judge? Or do you think of Him as a "meany," trickster, out to get us, like swapping a stone for bread or a serpent for fish? Of course not! Jesus portrays Him here as a "good Father." What is the importance of this picture to us, as we come to Him in prayer?

First, a little review. Remember when we looked at the Lord's Prayer? How did Jesus teach us to begin to speak with God? He said: "Our Father" (Mt 6:9). Do you realize what a wonderful privilege and relationship that is? Again, it is like my kids rushing to the door when I come home: "Papa! Daddy!" And when Jesus spoke about our need to relinquish our anxieties because God cares for us, how did He describe Him to us?

> Look at the birds of the air: they neither sow nor reap nor gather into barns, and yet your heavenly Father feeds them. Are you not of more value than they? (Mt 6:26).

As we saw then, a heart of worry betrays a lack of faith in *who God is to us*—more special than anything else, because He is our heavenly Father. And worry betrays a lack of faith in *who we are to Him*—more special than anything else, because we are His valuable children.

So, it is the tender relationship of knowing there is someone who is strong for you, who cares for you, who provides for you, so that you do not have to worry about the little things in life. For those of you who have had good, stable homes with loving fathers, did you ever have to worry about whether you would have food to eat, or whether your dad would love you, or want to spend time with you, or would hug you and bandage your knee, or that he would confront you fiercely if you ever defied him or disrespected your mother?

Second, I mention "good" here, because for some of you the mention of "father" does not naturally bring out connotations of goodness. Maybe you had a bad father, and that is how fathers are so often portrayed. But Jesus portrays for us how good our Father truly is (in 7:11). Regardless of how "good" we are, we are still "evil" compared to the utter goodness of the heavenly Father, compared to the standard of righteousness that He demands and freely offers to us by His grace, to all who will simply "ask"! So, if you had a good father, what a blessing! But "how much *more*" are we blessed by our heavenly Father, who is pure goodness!

Third, He gives good gifts (compare Jas 1:17). He is a good Father, and a good father always wants good things for his children. But when Jesus talks about "good things" here, it is "good" from God's perspective—which is often different, but better, than ours. What is the best gift you could ask for, that you can think of right now? If you are an adult, would it be a good husband or wife, a good car or house, a little extra spending money, etc.? If you are still a child, what is the best Christmas gift you want this year? When Jesus talked about this same issue in the Gospel of Luke (11:13), He said something very profound. In an otherwise verbatim statement, instead of "good things" Jesus said our heavenly Father gives us "the Holy Spirit." In other words, Jesus tells us what the best gift of all really is, and that He freely gives it. Imagine God's own presence within us and all that comes with that! This ought to re-orient our thinking, our attitude—even our asking and receiving—toward what Jesus had earlier said, "Seek first the kingdom of God and His righteousness" (Mt 6:33).

So, if we know we have a good Father, who gives "good things to those who ask Him" (7:11), should we not come to Him with confidence, knowing that He will open His arms to receive us, open His ears to hear us, and then get up and do everything within His power that is good and right for us?! Understanding *that* is a fundamental part of answering a looming question.

That looming question is this: What about unanswered prayer? That is the lingering question you are all probably asking—that I myself ask as I come to Jesus' words here. This passage does not seem to even allow that there will ever be such a thing; yet we have all probably experienced it, along with the disappointment. We have all probably had one or several major prayer concerns that have gone unanswered. We pray and pray, but never seem to get an answer—at least not the one we were praying for. But Jesus says we will! What do we do with this?

First, here Jesus, as in the rest of the Sermon, is painting in broad, attitude-adjusting strokes. His purpose is simply this: to orient us to *come to God with confidence, as a child to his father, knowing that He hears and readily answers.*

Second, in prayer we come not to a vending machine, but to a heavenly Father, who is supremely good Himself, who wants good things for us, and will indeed give them to us. But He does so from His perspective and in His time. For example, what sixteen-year-old does not want a fancy new car for his birthday? Many parents give just such a gift. But it seems to me that a better approach would be to let the new driver test his wings on more humble wheels.

Third, there are other Scriptures that help flesh out some of the puzzling details. For example, in James' letter, he writes:

> You do not have, because you do not ask. You ask and do not receive, because you ask wrongly, to spend it on your passions (Jas 4:2-3).

If we have examined our motives and are seeking Him first, we still must let God be God, once we realize that He always reserves the right to override. Yes, He is a good God whose love is ever with us. Yet His plans may be different—and better, in some strange-seeming way—than ours. Three chief examples come to mind: (1) Daniel's three friends, facing the fiery furnace because of their faith, issued the astounding statement that our God is *able* to deliver us and He *will* deliver us, but *if not*...(Dn 3:17-18); (2) The apostle Paul, wrestling with his thorn in the flesh, pleaded three times for the Lord to take it away; but God *answered,* no, "My grace is sufficient for you" (2 Cor 12:9); and (3) then there is our Lord Jesus Himself, pleading in the Garden for one thing—impassioned, persistent—and yet submitting Himself to the Father: "Your will be done" (Mt 26:42). For all of us who are His, it really is, "Father knows best." And it is the voice of faith that will own this, even as we wrestle with Him.

I began by saying that prayer is one of the most precious privileges and awesome resources of the Christian life. In prayer, we commune with the God of the universe. We talk in words and thoughts, and even the groans of our heart, with the one who fills all heaven and earth (Jer 23:24). The Eternal walks in time with me; the Infinite enters my space. The Holy and Beyond comes close to me in my struggles and failures— and yes, blatant sins—and offers the closeness of His presence and the cleansing of His grace. The Almighty cares for me. We are called into His presence and we can pray with confidence—confidence that He cares, He hears, and He answers. There are two very clear and simple reasons for this: it is because Jesus Himself summons us, and because we have a good heavenly Father. Who could ask for more?

THE GOLDEN RULE

(Matthew 7:12)

So whatever you wish that others would do to you,
do also to them,
for this is the Law and the Prophets.

WHEN we come to this verse, we come to the summary of the Sermon on the Mount, as we see by comparing Matthew 5:17, in which Jesus says that He has come to fulfill the Law and the Prophets, with *here*, "This *is* the Law and the Prophets." The Beatitudes and images of salt and light serve as the introductory material that lays the groundwork and sets the stage for who we must be in the world, and how we must function—out of a heart of humility and faith and paradox. The material that follows this pivotal verse serves to wrap it all up with a clear choice, in a binary way, and with a call to application—to *hear* and *do*.

Yet, as Jesus points out so clearly, it is more than just a summary of the Sermon; it is a summary of the Scriptures, made simple. This is what "the Law and the Prophets" means. Yet it is a call that is hard to heed because something keeps getting in the way.

SUMMARY OF THE SCRIPTURES

This verse usually goes by the well-known name, the Golden Rule which is a good life motto. But what does this Golden Rule mean?

First, it is *not*, "He who has the gold makes the rules" (as it is sometimes humorously twisted). This would be the way of the world, the way of *oppression* by the rich and powerful. But God hates oppression, regardless of who does it.

And it is *not*, "Do unto others *what* they have done unto you." This, again, is the way of the world, the way of *retaliation*, tit-for-tat. And it is certainly our instinct. But as Proverbs 24:29 clearly states: "Do not say, 'I will do to him as he has done to me; I will pay the man back for what he has done.'" A heart of retaliation is far from the heart of Christ.

It is also *more* than the so-called Silver Rule (that is, the Golden Rule, but framed in the negative). An early Christian document (the *Didache*) phrased it this way: "Do *not* do to another what you would not want done to you" (1:2). During Jesus' day, the Jewish Rabbi Hillel was challenged by a Gentile to give a summary of the Law in the short amount of time that this man could stand on one leg. Hillel responded: "What is hateful to you, do *not* do to anyone else. This is the whole Law; all the rest is commentary. Go and learn it" (b *Shabbath* 31a).[42] But then in either case, you could simply do *nothing* and fulfill the Law. Only Jesus, apparently, framed this summary rule in the positive—and thus made it more extensive and intensive, as we have seen Him do in His earlier citing of the Law.

Instead, the Golden Rule is *this*, as it is commonly re-phrased, "Do unto others as you would have them do unto you"; that is, "treat others the way you want to be treated." This is to be our governing principle and our life motto. Indeed, this is the way of Christ: the way of *love.* You see, Jesus calls us to something *more;* He calls us to love, and love is an action word.

But how does it summarize the Scriptures? Former President Bill Clinton made famous the phrase: "It depends on what the meaning of *is* is," and we laugh at that. Well, Jesus says that this Golden Rule *is* the Scriptures. What is the meaning of "is" here? The NIV renders it "sums up," which is not wrong, though "is" makes it stronger by framing it as equivalence.

Just as the apostle John said: "God is love" (1 John 4:8)—which fundamentally marks out God by that one thing, here Jesus says in essence that "God's Word is love." For the Golden Rule is basically love described—this is what love looks like in real life. It is love lived.

As we know from elsewhere, love is the fulfillment of the Law. When confronted with a test question from a trained lawyer, "Teacher, which is the great commandment in the Law?" Jesus replied:

---

42 Cited in D. A. Carson, Matthew 1-12, in *The Expositor's Bible Commentary*, ed. Frank E. Gaebelein (Grand Rapids: Zondervan, 1995), 187 (emphasis added).

You shall love the Lord your God with all your heart and with all your soul and with all your mind. This is the great and first commandment. And a second is like it: You shall love your neighbor as yourself. On these two commandments depend all the Law and the Prophets (Mt 22:36-40).

And similarly the apostle Paul says:

Owe no one anything, except to love each other, for the one who loves another has fulfilled the law. For the commandments, "You shall not commit adultery, You shall not murder, You shall not steal, You shall not covet," and any other commandment, are summed up in this word: "You shall love your neighbor as yourself." Love does no wrong to a neighbor; therefore love is the fulfilling of the law (Rom 13:8-10).

In this latter example, Paul lists some of the obvious ones from the Ten Commandments: If you love someone, you will not kill them; or You would not want someone to commit adultery with *your* wife—so do not do it with someone else's wife. But this love reaches to the entirety of the Scriptures; this is its core.

This equation of love with treating the other as you would want to be treated is also made explicit in the apostle Paul's marriage counseling: "Husbands, love your wives, as Christ loved the church and gave Himself up for her" (Eph 5:25). He explains: "For no one ever hated his own flesh, but nourishes and cherishes it, just as Christ does the church" (5:29). This love is illustrated in the Golden Rule.

We are living in an age when the thinking is to try to make all religions appear equivalent, especially trying to soften opinions regarding the hard edge of Islam. What is the core of Islam? By its very name and nature, it is "submission." What is the core of Christianity? By Jesus' own confession, it is "love." How is this *submission* in Islam lived out? Through a list of external rules and severe punishments (look at Sharia law). How is this *love* in Christianity lived out? Through the heart, internally driven, made alive and willing and able by the Holy Spirit. Do you see the contrast? Do you see the beauty? Do you see the better way?

So, the Golden Rule functions as the summary of the Scriptures, because it puts a handle on and gives a practical expression to the demand to love.

CENTER OF THE PROBLEM

But if it is so central and it is so clear, then why do we not keep it? Simply because something *else* is central in our lives: self and self-centeredness.

Self-centeredness is certainly the problem in our society, is it not? We live in a "me-first," materialistic, consumer-minded society. We do not really care how the other person feels, what the other person wants, even necessarily what is best or right. We want what *we* want, what makes us feel better or look good; and we end up with a society that has everything, and yet has lost its heart and soul. This mind-set has crept into the church as well.

What are the Christian books that sell? "Me"-books, such as for example, books about how you can be happy. What are the kind of sermons that bring in the crowds? "Me"-sermons, for example, about how you can have a more successful and fulfilling life. I am not saying these are all bad. But the church is being lulled into ineffectiveness and practically into irrelevance, because we have lost sight of the heart of the Christian life—which is *not me!* It is the cross—the place where "God demonstrates His own love for us" (Rom 5:8, NIV).

I will share an email story I received awhile back. Usually I quickly read and delete, but this one I found quite appropriate: A mother was preparing pancakes for her sons, Kevin, age five, and Ryan, age three; and the boys began to argue over who would get the first pancake. Their mother saw the opportunity for a moral lesson: "If Jesus were sitting here, He would say, 'Let my brother have the first pancake, I can wait.'" At which point Kevin turned to his younger brother and said, "Ryan, you be Jesus!" You see, he understood what Jesus would do; *he* just did not want to do likewise. This is something we struggle with from our earliest years and it never goes away: the struggle to truly love, to put the other person first before my wants, to treat him the way we would want to be treated. This we should do everyday, in everything.

Notice where this Golden Rule is placed. What leads up to it? It is certainly the grand climax of the whole sermon, but it also concludes the smaller section (7:1-12). It reads, "So…"—or you could also say,

"Therefore..." It thus caps what directly precedes it, and that is a call to humility based on our own sinfulness (7:2,5), and to the example of the goodness of God—even toward we who are evil and undeserving (7:11). If we first understand our own sinfulness and God's goodness, how much more will we be able to embrace, and begin to truly live, this great command!

But what does this mean in practice? If there is ever any question, ask yourself: "How would I want to be treated if I were in their shoes?" Step out of *self* and into *the other*, and then do that. This simple, basic rule—the rule of *love lived*—forces us to take a long, honest look at ourselves first, asking not "How does *he deserve* to be treated?" but "How would *I want* to be treated?"—which is usually with *grace*. Then we step out of ourselves and into the other in order to do that to the other person.[43]

So, for example, in my relationships: If I *do unto others what I would have them do unto me*, I would be genuine and gracious, not fake and petty. Who you see is who I am, and I am not looking at you with an eye toward judgment but an eye for grace. I would be kind and forgiving, not hateful and bitter. What a world of difference between them! And I would flee from put-downs and gossip and slander. Nothing destroys so quickly and easily as mean and cruel words, for "death and life are in the power of the tongue" (Prv 18:21). And yet, too often we do these things. Why? Because we do not follow this rule. And why? Because we are still too self-centered and not Christ-centered in our day-to-day lives.

Or in my workplace: If I *do unto others what I would have them do unto me*, I would conduct my business with honesty and integrity, whether as the boss or the employee. As a rule of thumb, give your work your best effort: a full day's labor for a full day's pay. Give your customers a good deal and do not go for the highest profit or try to manipulate them into buying something they do not really want or need. Put yourself in their shoes: this is the Golden Rule in real life.

We all have a rebellious spirit, since nobody naturally likes rules. But

---

43 This applies at the macro level as well. A pervading attitude of selflessness and self-restraint is an undergirding necessity for free institutions. If individuals or groups presumptuously impose themselves on others, resistance and escalation typically follow, and liberty is soon lost. Good manners (often referred to as "civility") are elemental to any civil government based in Christian liberty.

we all have to live with rules. There are good rules and there are bad rules. In either case, they are given by those in authority over us. Bad rules by bad leaders are a burden, discouraging, oppressing. But good rules by good leaders are life-giving and surprisingly freeing. Jesus is our good leader. He is our King, and He makes the rules. His rule is better than good; His rule is "golden" and His rule is love. On the cross, He shows us what that love looks like in its highest expression. For helpless and hopeless sinners, *do unto others as you would have them do unto you* meant that He freely gave Himself up to die for us. What would Jesus want if He were in my shoes? He would want forgiveness; He would want God's embrace. And that is just what He did for you and for me.

TWO ROADS DIVERGED

(Matthew 7:13-14)

Enter by the narrow gate.
For the gate is wide and the way is easy
that leads to destruction, and those who enter it are many.
For the gate is narrow and the way is hard
that leads to life, and those who find it are few.

IN Robert Frost's famous poem, "The Road Not Taken," he penned these words:

> Two roads diverged in a yellow wood,
> And sorry I could not travel both...
>
> Two roads diverged in a wood, and I—
> I took the one less traveled by,
> And that has made all the difference.[44]

Reflecting on these lines in light of the salvation that is offered in Christ and the decision that is called for from Christ, the late Larry Norman, known by many as "the father of Christian rock," mused in his classic song, "One Way":

> Two roads diverged in the middle of my life,
> I heard a wise man say.
> And I took the one less traveled by,
> And that's made the difference,
> every night and every day.[45]

---

44 First published in his *Mountain Interval*, 1916. Also found in Edward Connery Lathem, ed., *The Poetry of Robert Frost* (New York: Owl Books, 1979), 105. Although Frost was not a believer, the imagery he expresses can be applied in a Christian direction.

45 Larry Norman reflecting Frost's lines in his song "One Way," 1975, in the album, "In Another Land." Solid Rock Productions. All rights reserved. Used by permission.

Indeed, this is the imagery that our Lord places before us, even as He comes to the bold conclusion of His Sermon on the Mount (7:13-29). The Golden Rule functions as the capstone of His teaching, but He does not leave it there. Rather, Jesus brings His sermon to a close with a series of binary descriptions that call for decision; that we must either choose for or against Jesus, not just in what we say, but ultimately in what we do. He presents these options sequentially via the portraits of two gates, two trees, and two builders. In each case, Jesus underlines the significance and severity of the issue: for to choose against Jesus is to choose *destruction*. It is the way that "leads to destruction" (7:13) and to being "cut down and thrown into the fire" (7:19). It leads to a great and sudden collapse (7:27). It is not so much a threat as it is an intense warning, because in Jesus is the blessed way of life, and only those who follow in His way will have that life.

There are only two choices. This comes through most deeply in His first description of two gates and two ways which are the way of life or the way of destruction. Two roads diverge before each of us, and we must choose one.

The contrasts are stark: notice the series of polar opposites, set in direct contrast to one another. Each road has its own *entrance:* the narrow gate or the wide gate. Each road has its own *character:* the hard way or the easy way. Each road has its own *destination:* life or destruction.

ENTRANCE

FIRST, each road has its own entrance. It is entered through a doorway: the wide gate or the narrow gate. Although Jesus does not use the language here of "heaven and hell," the concept nonetheless is unmistakably clear. The gate that leads to hell is a wide gate, but the gate that leads to heaven is narrow. This statement was offensive in Jesus' own day, but is even more offensive in our present generation and modern milieu of religious pluralism, in which all roads are said to lead equally to God.

Whether that be the way of a nebulous "spirituality," or of being a good and loving person, or any number of sincerely held religious beliefs, the world in general considers that the gate is wide that leads to life. This opinion has certainly been popularized in recent years (with a Christian veneer) by the TV host Oprah Winfrey, and her objection to the exclusivity of Christ—an objection that much of our society shares. As Tim Keller notes in his recent book, *The Reason for God,* this is one of the most frequent objections to Christianity that he hears:

> During my nearly two decades in New York City, I've had numerous opportunities to ask people, "What is your biggest problem with Christianity? What troubles you the most about its beliefs or how it is practiced?" One of the most frequent answers I have heard over the years can be summed up in one word: *exclusivity.*[46]

But Jesus Himself says: "I am the way, and the truth, and the life. No one comes to the Father except through Me" (Jn 14:6). The testimony of Christ is that He is the only way to God. In this, He is indeed "narrow-minded."

Here it should be noted that, in a very real sense, the Bible is a book of bad news because it tells us that by ourselves we deserve to be damned before a holy God, and if left to ourselves...we would be damned. In the day of judgment, none of us can stand on our own merit, our own religion, our own sincerity. It would be like trying to skip a rock across the ocean, or to shoot an arrow to the moon—impossible! Some may be "better" than others (some rocks would skip farther, some arrows fly higher), but all would fall far "short of the glory of God" (Rom 3:23). *That* is the standard we miss in our sinfulness—and we all have it, especially at the level of the heart. No one can come close to God, unless God comes close to us, and He comes close to us in the cross. He is a God of grace who freely grants us what we do not deserve and could not earn.

You see, although the Bible *is* a book of bad news, it is also—and fundamentally—a book of good news: it tells us that "God so loved the world, that He gave His only Son, that whoever believes in Him should not perish but have eternal life" (Jn 3:16). This is the precious and costly love He displayed for us all when He sent Jesus to die on the cross for our sins. He shows us the width and wonder of His love in His wounded and outstretched arms.

The good news is this: that God has provided "a way"! To underscore this point, if there were any other equally valid way to God, then the cross

---

46 Timothy Keller, *The Reason for God: Belief in an Age of Skepticism* (New York: Dutton, 2008), 3 (italics his).

would not be a good example and Christ would not be a great teacher. If there were any other way (think about it!), then the cross would be absolutely *unnecessary*, and Christ *a fool!* [47] So, if you want to get to heaven (to enter *life*, as Jesus calls it), you have to come through Him. There is no other gate that will lead you there. The only other option (and one that covers a wide expanse) leads only to destruction.

CHARACTER

SECOND, each road has its own character, its own "look and feel": the easy way or the hard way. The term here used for "easy" (εὐρύχωρος) refers to how broad and spacious it is, and thus how easy to travel on; the word for "hard" is its opposite (τεθλιμμένη), and speaks of how compressed or restricted the road is. But the term also denotes tribulation. Thus the hard way is not only one that is narrow, it is also one that is fraught with affliction.

The way that leads to destruction is easy. This has been a cause of questioning for God's people throughout the ages. For is not the way of obedience the way of blessing? And so why is it that so often it is the wicked who prosper? Even the psalmist struggled with this very thing:

> But as for me, my foot had almost stumbled,
> my steps had nearly slipped.
> For I was envious of the arrogant
> when I saw the prosperity of the wicked
> (Ps 73:2-3).

But as he wrestles with his faith, the psalmist comes to realize that the end of the wicked is destruction, and the portion of the pure in heart is the presence of God forever. This is the same contrast and destiny that Jesus describes here.

The way that leads to life is hard. For as Jesus tells us, the Christian life is the way of the cross—of self-denial, of rejection and persecution. It is still the most blessed way, with the most blessed end, but it is characterized by difficulty and opposition nonetheless. Jesus Himself sets the

---

47 And we would be fools to follow Him (compare the apostle Paul's pointed words in 1 Cor 15:14-19).

example: "Who for the joy that was set before Him endured the cross" (Heb 12:2). When Jesus issued His repeated calls to discipleship—to believe in and follow Him—He did so in such demanding terms as: leave everyone behind, love everyone less than God, even lose your own life (see Mt 8:21-22; 10:37-39)! The Christian life is not for the faint of heart, and we do a grave disservice if we paint a rosy picture or proclaim that all you have to do is accept Jesus and everything will be fine. This is an all-too-common practice among American pastors and prosperity preachers whose focus is more on self-motivation, empowerment, and betterment, and very little on the call of self-denial, the call of true discipleship. In fact, the cross is more or less an addendum to much of what is preached. It is mentioned but not central, nice but not essential. However, the call of Christ is the call of the cross. And the call of the cross is life… through death.

> If anyone would come after Me, let him deny himself and take up his cross and follow Me. For whoever would save his life will lose it, but whoever loses his life for My sake will find it (Mt 16:24-25).

DESTINATION

And THIRD, each road has its own destination, its own end point which is either destruction or life. This contrast in ways and destinies is a common theme carried over from the Old Testament (see, for example, Ps 1). Most notably, however, at the close of that great renewal of the Law for the younger generation of Israelites poised to enter the Promised Land, God (through Moses) presents this dramatic contrast and call to decision:

> See, I have set before you today life and good, death and evil. If you obey the commandments of the LORD your God that I command you today, by loving the LORD your God, by walking in His ways, and by keeping His commandments and His statutes and His rules, then you shall live and multiply, and the LORD your God will bless you in the land that you are entering to take possession of it. But if your heart turns away, and you will not hear, but are drawn away to worship other

gods and serve them, I declare to you today, that you shall surely perish. You shall not live long in the land that you are going over the Jordan to enter and possess. I call heaven and earth to witness against you today, that I have set before you life and death, blessing and curse. Therefore choose life, that you and your offspring may live (Dt 30:15-19).

Jesus brings this call to decision directly to Himself, and He brings this contrast in destinations to its ultimate goal: heaven or hell. Jesus says: If you enter through the wide gate and take the easy way, you will find nothing but destruction in the end. But if you enter through the narrow gate (Jesus Himself) and take the hard way (the way of the cross), you will find what truly leads to eternal life.

But how many choose the wide gate and the easy way... and end in destruction! As Jesus frames it in one final contrast: it is many versus few. Many choose the path of destruction; few choose the way of life. For who would naturally prefer the hard way, and who would want to swim against the stream, to walk a path apart from their peers? Two roads diverge: they go in completely different directions, and have completely different destinations. But Jesus calls us all to one decision: "Enter by the narrow gate" (7:13). That is where His heart is for us. But where is ours? Is it for Him?

This is the first of His binary images, and it conveys the message starkly. There are only two options. There is no middle ground. Like other binary examples in our daily life: an electric switch is either on or off. In computer language, it is either 1 or 0. So here it is a binary decision. Two roads diverge, and we can only choose one. Let us choose wisely.

21

THE PERIL OF
FALSE PROFESSION

(Matthew 7:15-23)

Beware of false prophets, who come to you in sheep's clothing
but inwardly are ravenous wolves.
You will recognize them by their fruits.
Are grapes gathered from thornbushes, or figs from thistles?
So, every healthy tree bears good fruit,
but the diseased tree bears bad fruit.
A healthy tree cannot bear bad fruit,
nor can a diseased tree bear good fruit.
Every tree that does not bear good fruit
is cut down and thrown into the fire.
Thus you will recognize them by their fruits.

Not everyone who says to me, "Lord, Lord,"
will enter the kingdom of heaven,
but the one who does the will of My Father who is in heaven.
On that day many will say to Me, "Lord, Lord, did we not prophesy
in Your name, and cast out demons in Your name,
and do many mighty works in Your name?"
And then will I declare to them,
"I never knew you;
depart from Me, you workers of lawlessness."

W HAT a sobering passage!
On a lighter note: How many of you have seen the first Ice Age
movie? It was one of my favorites, and I laughed more than all the other

kids in the theatre. Before the start of every movie, the rating appears: for example, PG (parental guidance), followed by the reason for that rating. And I find it quite humorous that the notice at the beginning of that movie was: PG, for "mild peril." What a choice of words to place together! If this passage of Scripture were rated, it would have to be marked "warning: *severe* peril." Here we need to take notice, for the consequences of presuming or ignoring this warning are eternal and horrible.

We continue here with the conclusion to Jesus' Sermon on the Mount, a conclusion that He drives home with a series of binary descriptions, each with their call to decision (7:13-27, two gates, two trees, two builders). In this central section of His concluding call, Jesus addresses two common things that many people say and think, issuing two very solemn warnings to us all.

SPEAKING FOR GOD?

The first solemn warning is this: *There are many who say they speak for God, but they do not* (7:15-20).

Know Them by Their Fruits

Jesus calls them "false prophets" (7:15). What does that mean? Basically, a prophet is someone who is set apart to speak for God. In our day, we could call them pastors, ministers, religious leaders, evangelists, witnesses. But Jesus warns us that there are some who claim to speak for God that are "false"; that is, they neither know Him nor speak for Him. But how can we tell the difference between the false and the true? The answer may surprise you.

You may find it difficult at first to tell the difference. As Jesus describes them, false prophets are wolves in sheep's clothing. They might look like sheep and smell like sheep; but they have sharp teeth and do not want to eat grass. So, you might not see the difference between the false and the true right away or by a casual glance, until you take a closer look and see the underlying the nature of what they really say, do, and want.

Likewise in the next picture Jesus paints, you cannot tell from a distance if a tree is good or bad, or bears good or bad fruit, until you look closer. From a distance, by outside appearances, all you see is, for example, an apple tree with apples on it. You would not know that the tree is sick and the fruit is rotten. It is only when you look closely that you can see and judge its fruit.

This is where Jesus underscores that we will know them by their fruits. Twice He emphasizes this as the way of discerning the true spokesman for God from the false, as the framing that begins and ends His fruit tree illustration: "You will recognize them by their fruits" (7:16 and 20). This is another one of Jesus' common illustrations from daily life—because they are easy to see and easy to understand. So what are we to understand about false prophets from fruit trees?

One: you can tell the *identity* of the tree by its fruit (7:16). Grapes do not grow on blackberry bushes. If you are seeing grapes, you know it is a grapevine. So, too, if you are seeing or hearing something that is definitely not "Jesus" as we find Him in the Word, then you know that person is not a true spokesman for Jesus. We will look at what some of those things might be in a moment.

And two: you can tell the *quality* of the tree by its fruit (7:17-18). If the fruit is plump and rich, you know the tree is healthy; but if the fruit is small and blemished or foul tasting, or if eating it makes you ill, you know something is wrong with the tree. So, look at the results in their life or the lives of the followers of someone who says he speaks for God. Is he fostering the fruit of the Spirit: "love, joy, peace..." (Gal 5:22)? Is he spreading "the aroma of Christ" (2 Cor 2:15)? Then he is a vigorous tree and a true prophet. But if he is spreading selfishness and divisiveness, then you know he is a diseased tree.

Then there is the threat of judgment: worthless trees are "cut down and thrown into the fire" (7:19; see Mt 3:10). This is the very real—and very scary—threat of damnation for those who pretend to be true believers and Christian leaders, but are not and are leading others down a path of extreme peril with them. We will see how this threat is ramped up in 7:23. God is the gardener, and He inspects His orchard; we can fool others, but we cannot fool Him—because He reads the heart. And He has a judgment day set. None of us knows when that day will come—but it will come, maybe today, maybe tomorrow. Whether the Lord returns, or you get hit by the proverbial dump truck—we all have a date with death and destiny. The question is: Are you ready to stand for inspection? Are you ready to meet your Maker? He will either save you *from* your sins, which is beautiful beyond words, or judge you *for* your sins, which is terrifying beyond description.

The Fruits of a False Prophet

So, what are the fruits of a false prophet? Two things, both of which are tempting. It looks good—as when Eve in the Garden saw that the fruit was good and pleasing and desirable (Gn 3:6). But it was really bad, and it only led to bad things. That is seen both in the fruit of their lips and the fruit of their lives, in what they say and what they do. The fruit of *false doctrine* and the fruit of *false deeds* generally go hand in hand. The false doctrine here, especially, is the denial of the narrow gate and the hard way (7:14)—where they speak "nicely" and yet skirt the center, avoiding the cross. As to their false deeds, Jesus calls them "workers of lawlessness" (7:23), who do not do "the will of My Father" (7:21). And the Father's will is not seen in flashy religious displays, like casting out demons and other mighty works (7:22). It is seen in "the obedience of faith" and "faith working through love" (Rom 1:5; Gal 5:6).

These are the same two things that were common to the false prophets of the Old Testament: speaking what was comfortable for acceptance or for money and leading in immorality. For example, God says through Jeremiah:

> Everyone is greedy for unjust gain; from prophet to priest, everyone deals falsely. They have healed the wound of My people lightly, saying, "Peace, peace," when there is no peace (Jer 8:10b-11).

The people were sinning in obvious ways, but instead of calling them to repentance, their leaders were saying: "Everything is OK; God is not going to judge you." This is healing the wound lightly. It is like putting a coat of paint over rotten wood or like putting a Band-Aid® over a malignant skin cancer. It might sound nice, it might look good. But there is no peace in the midst of sin. There is no comfort where there is not true faith and repentance.

These are the same two things we keep hearing and seeing. How many religious leaders do you hear today proclaiming a narrow gate and a hard way? Or do you hear instead a wide gate and an easy way? Many preach that there are many paths to God. Some preach a prosperity "gospel." Too many preach accommodation to the culture. Especially in vogue today are issues of sexuality, where pornography is OK, homosexuality is OK, everything is all right if it is "the real you" or makes you happy and does not hurt anybody. But where, then, is the cross? Where, then, is repentance from sin? Where, then, is humility? Where, then, is true grace through the love of God expressed in Christ's suffering and dying in the place of sinners like you and me? The apostle Paul said to young pastor Timothy these same two things: "Watch your life and doctrine closely" (1 Tm 4:16, NIV).

So, who do we need to watch out for? It is not just the obvious ones like Muslim clerics, who speak for a false god. Rather, this is primarily a warning for the church, and it is directed at those who pretend to speak for the true God. Like Jesus' opening words here, the apostle Paul warned the Ephesian *elders* that wolves would arise from their own midst (Acts 20:29-30). And what do wolves do? They eat sheep; they divide and destroy the flock.

It is not the cult figures like Jim Jones and David Koresh that are the most dangerous. It is others whom that we might not notice at first. They draw a huge following by lulling people into a false sense of security or toward the false god of self. They have money as their focus, are in it for themselves rather than for the cause of Christ, and they promote and even practice immorality. They gloss over issues that are clearly sin, thus making the gate wider than Christ and the way easier than the cross. These are the false prophets, and Jesus says, "Beware."

But the next warning gets even closer, because it reaches to the level of each of us.

GOING TO HEAVEN?

The second warning is even more severe: *There are many who think they will go to heaven, but they will not* (7:21-23). We have all heard the polls: a majority of Americans claim to be Christians, and yet in many cases their attitudes and actions are no different than the non-Christians. This is unpleasant to hear and to say: but there are many people who think they are going to heaven, who will get a horrible surprise on judgment day.

What They Profess

Strikingly, they profess to know Jesus. They say, "Lord, Lord"—but that is not enough (7:21). To say "Jesus is Lord" is the basic Christian confession. Only Christians say it, and it is this statement that marks out a Christian (Rom 10:9). They do not just say, "Lord"; they say, "Lord, Lord"—which denotes fervency. There may even be a sense of self-deception among professing Christians. They honestly believe that they are going to heaven; and it will be a horrifying shock when they find out they are not. Ask random persons on the street, ask random persons in the pew: "Do you believe in heaven and hell?" and then, "Do you think you are going to heaven?" I would be willing to wager that nine out of ten who answered "yes" to the first also answer "yes" to the second. Too few people today are concerned that they might be going to hell or are afraid of going to hell as a consequence of their sins, or are aware of their desperate need for a Savior. We have lulled them into a dangerous sleep; the church has shirked its duty.

And they do lots of good things for God—but that is not enough either (7:22). Notice all the great things they do: they "prophesy" (speak for God—even *preach* for God); they "cast out demons" (what could be harder than that?); and they "do many mighty works" (which would include both miracles and charities—like praying for someone to be healed or spearheading a ministry to victims of AIDS; and what could be better than that?). And notice, too, that it is all being done "in Jesus' name" (stated three times). In such organizations as some liberal ecumenical church councils, there is a lot of this going on: "Lord, Lord" and "in Your name." But if their practice and fruit are not according to Scripture, those of faith should discern that something is missing.

So, what *is* enough? How much more does God want? I am called by His name; I call on His name. But it is not just words that God wants; and not just good—even great—religious things. It is a will aligned with His, which means a heart that has been changed by Him: it is "the one who does the will of My Father who is in heaven" (7:21b). Going back to "Lord" again: this is indeed—and rightly—the basic Christian confession. But too often we bat it back and forth, as a word with no real meaning. We say it freely, without knowing what we are saying. But "lord" means "master" (the closest thing we probably have in our culture now is "boss"—though that is far too weak). If He is my Master, then I am His servant. That means that I *belong* to Him, and that I will *obey* Him. My will is no longer mine. It is only His will that matters. You see how this now cuts so deeply against the grain of so much of American religion?

What Jesus Will Profess

But equally striking, Jesus will profess, "I never knew you" (7:23). These would be to us the scariest words ever spoken, and these are from the lips of Jesus! It should shake us to the core. This is the peril of false profession: "You claimed to know Me, but I never knew *you*; depart from Me."

These are scary words that "many" will hear (7:22). It grieves me to even think about such a thing! There are certainly many in our culture who will hear them and be surprised (recall Mt 7:13b). These days, there are religious and community centers with popular "programs for spiritual living" that draw many participants; I know of some that promote a lot of "spiritual" things and try to take some good ideas from all the world's religions. However, what this does is feed the self and starve Jesus.

There will be people in our churches—perhaps even some in your own church (God forbid!) who come week after week to worship in the pews, to sit and hear the Word of God's salvation in the cross of Christ...and yet they have not really let it take root in their own hearts and lives. You may presume to be saved; you assume that because you are good, you come to church, you believe in God and Jesus, that you are (of course!) going to heaven. But even the demons believe in Him at this level—and tremble (Jas 2:19). Where will these demons end up?

So, what do we need to do about this? Ignore it? No—to our peril! Should we always be second-guessing our salvation? Again, no—there is such a thing as assurance of salvation. But the call of this passage on each of our hearts is this: "Examine yourselves, to see whether you are in the faith" (2 Cor 13:5). For example, when you sin, does it bother you? Or, are you more concerned about your own will than doing His will? Jesus came to earth as God in the flesh, to live a life of perfect obedience to the Father, to die on the cross for our sins as our *Substitute*, and to be raised from the dead as our living Lord and Savior. Are you trusting in Him for heaven, or are you counting on your own relative goodness to get you there? God's standard is not goodness, it is *perfection*—the glory of absolute holiness. Examine yourself. Have you ever truly done this? If not, do not delay; do it now: "Now is the day of salvation" (2 Cor 6:2). For many of us, tomorrow may never come. The Scripture says that after death, there is the judgment (Heb 9:27). On that day, what will Jesus say to you: Will it be "Depart from Me" (7:23), or will it be "Enter thou into the joy of thy Lord" (Mt 25:21, KJV)?

NIKE CHRISTIANS

(Matthew 7:24-29)

*"Everyone then who hears these words of Mine and does them
will be like a wise man who built his house on the rock.
And the rain fell, and the floods came,
and the winds blew and beat on that house,
but it did not fall, because it had been founded on the rock.
"And everyone who hears these words of Mine and does not do them
will be like a foolish man who built his house on the sand.
And the rain fell, and the floods came,
and the winds blew and beat against that house,
and it fell, and great was the fall of it."*

*And when Jesus finished these sayings,
the crowds were astonished at His teaching,
for He was teaching them as one who had authority,
and not as their scribes.*

WHAT was the Nike slogan? "Just do it." And that is not bad, for this is what Jesus calls us to do. Jesus wants us all to be "Nike Christians." That means not to just study the Word, discuss the Word, debate the Word—even love the Word. We are not called to just *"hear"* it; we are called to hear the Word and then *"do"* it. This should be our perpetual response to the authority of Christ.

THE STENCH OF AUTHORITY

Authority has a bad smell in our day and age. No one wants to come under someone else's authority. Everyone wants to be his own authority—or at least to pick and choose. This passage has the *stench* of authority all over it. It is introduced at the very beginning when Jesus says, "these words *of Mine*" (in 7:24, and again in 7:26). It is capped at its conclusion when Jesus "finished these sayings" (7:28, literally *"these words"), and* the resulting comment was that the crowds were astonished at His authority.

With these words we have come to the conclusion, not only of the Sermon on the Mount, but also of the first major portion of the Gospel proper. Five times in his Gospel, Matthew uses the phrase, "When Jesus finished… " or "When Jesus had finished… " (7:28; see Mt 11:1; 13:53; 19:1; 26:1). Each time it comes at the close of a series of Jesus' teachings and serves as a significant turning point in the development of Matthew's Gospel. And the first turning point is this issue of authority. We can see meaning even in the structure of the how the teachings are written down.

And the focal issue of obedience is to hear…*and do it,* which underscores this very question of authority as well. Who calls the shots? And what am I going to do about it? As Jesus closes His sermon, it is this issue of authority and our response to His authority that hits us all. So, let us look at these two questions.

AUTHORITY CONFRONTS

The first question we all must face is: *Who calls the shots?* This is where the issue of authority *confronts* us.

In these final verses (7:28-29), we see the authority of Jesus set in stark contrast to the authority of the scribes—those who devoted their lives to studying, explaining, and hand-copying the Scriptures. If you have to write something out by hand over and over, you tend to learn it very well. I am reminded of when I got in trouble in Mr. Vander Mey's class at my Christian grade school, and had to write "500 lines" to turn in to him the next day: "I will not talk in class, I will not talk in class… " (ah, pleasant memories). The scribes were the Bible experts of that day, like our seminary professors or pastors; and the crowds noticed and were astonished at the difference.

But what marked the difference? In a nutshell, three things: (1) The scribes were fond of quoting "the words of Rabbi so-and-so"; but Jesus said, "these words *of Mine*." (2) The scribes were fond of endlessly debating; but Jesus said, "whoever hears and *does* them." And (3) the scribes made the Scriptures complicated and hard to do, but you *could* still *do* what they said. But Jesus made the Scriptures clear in all their force, and *impossible* to do—except by an act of divine grace (see Mt 5:20).

Here is an example: The Mishnah records much of the teaching and traditions of the scribes, many of which go back to the time of Jesus. Some of the matters were significant, and some of them were just silly. For instance, in the discussion on "purities," it talks about rules for someone who became unclean through touching a corpse (good so far), who happened to have a fig in his mouth. If, in eating this fig with unclean hands, he pokes his hand into his mouth—the debate goes like this: Rabbi Meir declares the fig unclean. Rabbi Judah declares the fig clean. Rabbi Yose says, "If he turned over the fig in his mouth, it is unclean. If he did not turn it over, it is clean" (*Kelim* 8:10).[48] How could anyone be seriously concerned about such a dubious difference?

But Jesus puts the focus squarely on Himself. Earlier in the sermon, He had gone through a series of internalized and intensified re-statements of the Law of God, each introduced by the phrase: "You have heard that it was said…*but I say to you*" (for example, Mt 5:21-22 and 27-28). Thus, He boldly put Himself on the same level as the original lawgiver: God! And no authority gets higher than that. As He comes to a close, He brings the issue back to us once again: "Everyone then who hears *these words of Mine* and does them" (7:24). Ultimately, it is not what "so-and-so says," it is what Jesus says, and this is where it hits each of us.

So, what about us? We look at them, and think: "How silly and distracted the rabbis' dispute is from what is really important." But we, too, have our "Rabbi so-and-so's." We want to know what "so-and-so" says, more than what Jesus says. We read their works to see what they think, instead of the Bible. We have a tendency to look, for example, to John Calvin (for Reformed Christians), or to Rick Warren (for the broader Evangelical world), or to Pope Benedict (for the Catholics), instead of to the word of Christ, Who is the sole authority in our life. As Colossians 3:16 says, "Let the word *of Christ* dwell in you richly."

It is not just "the words of Christ in red" (as some liberals are fond of citing); it is the whole Bible. Some people say that since Jesus did not speak explicitly about such-and-such an issue (like abortion and gay

---

48 See Jacob Neusner, *The Mishnah: A New Translation* (New Haven, CT: Yale University Press, 1988), 908.

marriage), that means it is not that important to Him or to God. But God is not divided; He speaks with one voice. The same Jesus who walked this earth is eternally with the Father, and the Holy Spirit of God has inspired it all (see 2 Tm 3:16).

So, who or what is the authority over me? If it is anything other than Jesus speaking through the Scriptures, then I am standing on shaky and unstable ground.

AUTHORITY COMPELS

It is not enough to ask, Who calls the shots? We must also ask ourselves, *What am I going to do about it?* This is where the issue of authority *compels* us. We are all faced with the decision, How am I going to respond to the authority of Christ?

Jesus explains this decision with another common illustration: two builders on two foundations; a wise builder on the rock, and a foolish builder on the sand (7:24-27). Let me ask three simple questions:

First, what makes the wise man wise, and the foolish man foolish? The difference is hearing versus hearing *and doing*. As James 1:22 says, "Be doers of the word, and not hearers only." But this does not come naturally. What comes naturally is, "in one ear and out the other." Doing is a decision; and obedience must be learned. Anyone who has had children understands this.

Second, what is this likened to? It is likened to a foundation on rock versus sand. Just listening to Jesus, admiring Jesus—even being "astonished at His teaching" (7:28); reading your Bible, coming to church, saying you are a Christian: all of this is nothing more or better than building your dream house right on an ocean beach—on the sand itself. Lovely place, great view, step right out onto the sand and surf; and you do not have to climb down any difficult steps or walk an extra quarter mile—like those who build their houses further in on firmer ground. When the sun is shining and all is well, no problem, life is good.

Third, so where is the problem? What makes the difference? The difference is when life is *not* good, which happens to all of us, and especially when it happens all-of-a-sudden. It is only in the storms of life that our wisdom and folly are tested and revealed. In the land of Israel, they would have torrents of rain that turned dry creek-beds into rushing rivers. In

Texas, where my wife is from, they call these "gully-washers." Only a fool would build his house there. But that is the picture we are to see.

So, what about you? Where are you building your house? On what foundation are you betting your life? The storms of life will come. And you will either stand through them, or be destroyed by them. For example, the storm of marital discord: what if your closest relationship and the core of your life is being torn in two. Or what if you suddenly are involved in a traffic accident, or experience the death of a loved one—horrible to even consider! Or perhaps you face the storm of financial ruin, of your security in life turned upside-down. Or maybe you even struggle with the storm of disillusionment or doubt. Who does not wrestle with these? Then there are our perpetual struggles with sinful tendencies, our fallen frailties, our unmet needs. There is the relentless storm of aging or the sudden onset of illness or disease, and all the ravages of decreased function and helplessness and loneliness that come along with it. All of these are but shadows of the storm that will come on judgment day.

The storms of life will come, and the obedient life is the only one that will weather the storm both now and then. Why? Because in hearing His words and *doing* them, I show that I am truly *trusting* Him—in His authority over my life and over the storms of life—rather than trusting in myself or living for myself. Only then am I standing on the *rock*, and that Rock is Christ.

So, what are you standing on now? Who are you trusting in to support and see you through all those things that are far larger and harder than anything you can handle? Are you trusting in your own strength? It will fail. Are you trusting in your own goodness? It is frail. Or have you built your house—your life—on Jesus? He is a mighty rock and a solid foundation. No storm is stronger than He.

JUST DO IT!

Back in 1989, Nike produced a television commercial for hiking shoes that was shot in Kenya using some local Samburu tribesmen. As the spot closed, the camera focused in on one of the tribesmen speaking in his native Maa language. And as he was speaking, the Nike slogan, "Just do it," appeared on the screen. It was beautiful. But there was one problem: an anthropologist at the University of Cincinnati who knew the language, revealed that the Kenyan really said, "I don't want these. Give me big shoes" ("Mayieu kuna. Ijooki inamuk sapukin"). A Nike spokeswoman replied, "We thought nobody in America would know what he said."[49]

Setting humor aside, this is what separates—at a very practical level— the true Christian from the simply nominal Christian: How do I respond to Christ's authority in my life? When He says, "Jump," do I say, "How high?" When He says "Do this," do I brush it off as though it is just a suggestion, or find something else that I want to do instead? Jesus wants us all to be "Nike Christians," and not to be sending mixed messages, as the old commercial unwittingly did—and as so many American Christians do, who may be Christian in name, but not in their everyday attitudes and actions. Rather, if you know what Jesus says, and the opportunity for obedience is placed before you, then...*Just do it!*

---

49 *The New York Times.* "If the Shoe Doesn't Fit." 15 February 1989, A26.

SCRIPTURE INDEX

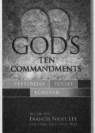

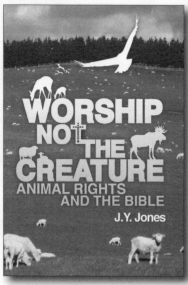

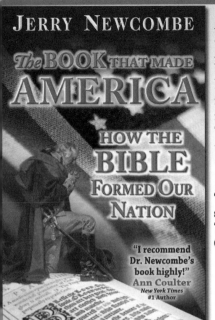

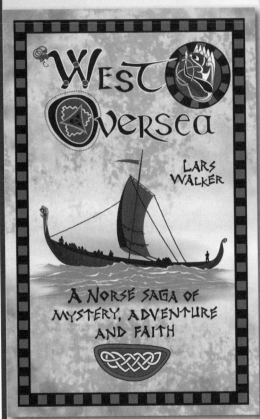